SPUNBONDED TEXTILE AND STITCH

LUTRADUR, EVOLON AND OTHER DISTRESSABLES

SPUNBONDED TEXTILE AND STITCH

LUTRADUR, EVOLON AND OTHER DISTRESSABLES

Wendy Cotterill

BATSFORD

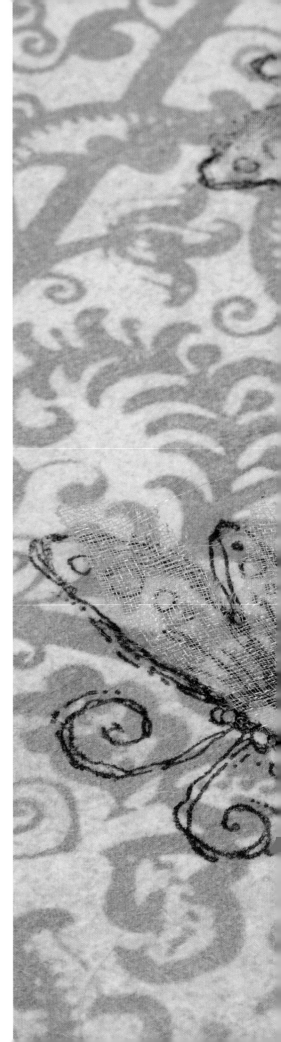

'Things to their best perfection come,
Not all at once; but, some and some.'
George Wither (1635)

First published in the United Kingdom in 2011 by
Batsford
10 Southcombe Street
London W14 0RA

An imprint of Anova Books Company Ltd

Lutradur® and Evolon® are registered trademarks of Freudenberg
Nonwovens Group; Tyvek® is a registered trademark of E.I. du Pont
de Nemours and Company and its affiliates; Kunin™ is a registered
trademark of Foss Manufacturing Company, LLC.

ISBN-13: 9781849940016

A CIP catalogue record for this book is available from the
British Library.

20 19 18 17 16 15 14 13 12 11
10 9 8 7 6 5 4 3 2 1

Reproduction by Rival Colour Ltd, UK
Printed by Craft Print International Ltd, Singapore

This book can be ordered direct from the publisher at the
website: www.anovabooks.com, or try your local bookshop.

PAGE 1: This book is made from paper Tyvek, printed and coloured
with everyday paints and dyes (see page 36).

PAGE 2: Fabric Tyvek has been coloured using an inkjet printer, then quilted, cut and
stitched into small squares. Copper pins hold the squares in place on mount board.

RIGHT: Evolon was printed with a digital image. Rubber-stamped dragonflies
were then overlaid with organza and cut and fused with a soldering iron.

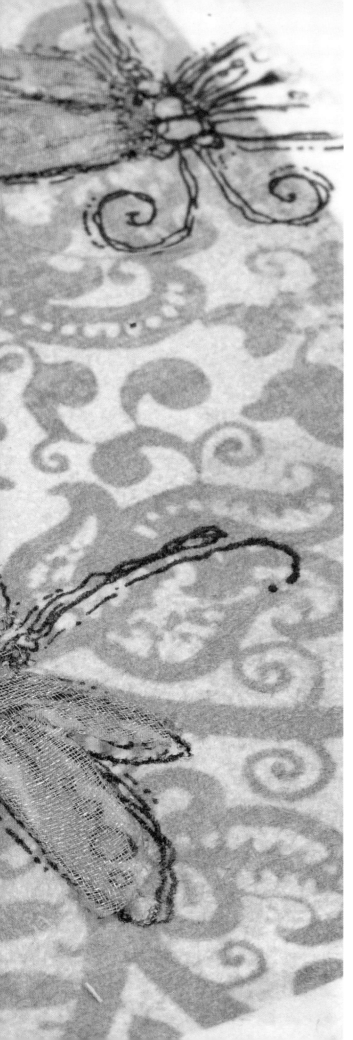

CONTENTS

INTRODUCTION

'Where to start?' is probably the first question that comes to mind. When finding yourself in a toolshed filled with equipment, the biggest barrier to accessing and using the tools is the fear of the unknown. But you need to sweep all of that aside, pick up a soldering iron, plug it in, place it on or near a piece of fabric and see what happens. Educators call this 'experiential learning' – it is how we all learn, and how barriers are broken down. Not many of the tools or fabrics in this book are manufactured for the purpose of creating decorative pieces of work and, likewise, none of the techniques have been handed down by previous generations. However, hopefully you can find a few new ideas to inspire and add to your repertoire. We are the pioneers.

Spunbonded textiles are non-woven fabrics – that is, fabric that is neither woven nor knitted. Non-wovens are typically manufactured by laying small, spun, extruded polymer filaments down in a web on a continuous conveyor belt (in a similar way to paper fibres being laid down on a paper machine). The fibres are then bonded together in one of three ways: mechanically, with the fibres being intertwined by water jets or needles; chemically, using binders such as latex emulsion, solution polymers or binder fibres; or thermally, by calendering the web through heated rollers. The table on page 124 gives the exact specifications of the different types of spunbonded textiles.

This book explores the creative potential of these new fabrics and demonstrates a range of simple yet inspiring techniques that can be incorporated into your textiles.

RIGHT: Crystal spunbonded polyester is exceptionally fine and, when heat-distressed, exposed areas will melt away quite easily. This example shows how this effect, combined with a stronger coloured fabric placed underneath, creates both dimension and texture.

TOOLS & TECHNIQUES

One of the most popular trends in creative textiles in the 21st century has been the way embroiderers and quilters have started using synthetic fibres of spunbonded construction in their work. It began with synthetic organzas and voiles being distressed with a heat tool or cut with a soldering iron. Subsequently, spunbonded fabrics that were originally developed for use in industry – including automotive manufacturing, construction and medical services – have been adapted for use by textile artists.

EQUIPMENT

Much like the fabrics themselves, equipment can be appropriated from industry, such as soldering irons, or from office equipment, such as desktop computers and printers. Some are now being manufactured specifically for the craft market, while others continue to be appropriated. No matter. Never stop investigating new possibilities in unexpected places.

SOLDERING IRON

To the uninitiated, a soldering iron for the purposes of distressing fabric is not used in conjunction with solder – it is merely a very hot-tipped tool for cutting. Soldering irons developed for craft use are usually 18 watts and will cut and melt most synthetic fibres. A 30-watt or a heat-variable tool can be helpful for use with fabrics that are constructed from denser fibres (such as Evolon) or are a thicker construction (such as felt). A hotter iron will cut through layers or thicker fabric more quickly and evenly.

Soldering irons developed for industrial use operate at far higher temperatures but lower-temperature irons can be easily adapted for use in textiles, although the ones with interchangeable tips are generally larger and more expensive. A craft soldering iron has many more specialist tips available, which simply screw into the wand and range from fine needle-tipped points to large bosses and large flat tips that can be used as a gem embellisher or quilting iron.

IRON

Domestic irons are perfectly adequate for the job of transferring transfer dyes, although they must not be used on a steam setting. Steam irons can also leave circular impressions of the foot-plate steam vents on your fabric, and therefore must be moved constantly when pressing to avoid this. A laundry press can achieve a much more even finish, but again must not be used in conjunction with steam.

HEAT TOOL

These are commonly referred to as heat guns, but should not be confused with a paint-stripper heat gun. Craft heat tools are relatively low wattage and are now commonly available with a twin-speed setting. Faster-flowing hot air can melt some fabrics, such as nappy liner, too quickly. A slower speed of heat helps to control the rate at which the fabric melts and burns. Heat tools are available either as a tube or a gun shape.

INKJET PRINTER

What you really need to know about inkjet printers is how to identify which type of ink yours uses – dye- or pigment-based – and the advantages of each. Generally, older printers and those that use a combination single cartridge for the three colours will be dye-based.

Refill packs purchased from supermarkets and stationers tend to be dye-based. The simple practical test is to take a print out from your printer, allow it dry, and then plunge it into water. If the ink runs it is probably dye-based. The relevant point here is that the colours will run – in other words, it is not permanent – and that is what you need to know.

If inks are promoted as bleed-proof, run-proof, or fade-proof, and have a single cartridge of each colour, they are probably pigment-based. Again, the test is that if the ink does not run when placed in water, it is probably pigment-based.

On the face of it, you may consider that a dye-based ink is not desirable but, as demonstrated within the main body of this book, dye-based inks can be discharged with water and used in combination with discharge techniques.

LASER PRINTER

There are two main relevant points about laser printers. First, a laser printer uses toner to create images. Toner is, in essence, a powdered plastic that is heat set onto paper. It is largely impervious to water, but will re-melt if enough heat is reapplied. This can be used to advantage – see page 24, creating text 'images' using transfer dyes.

Second, many scanner/printer/copiers that are commonly being referred to as 'photocopiers' are actually inkjet printers. For the purposes of the techniques described in this book, a photocopy is a laser-toner copy. Many people have access to laser printers in their office and many corner shops or post offices still have laser photocopiers for public use.

PHOTO-EDITING SOFTWARE

There are many pieces of software that will enable you to digitally alter an image, but the industry standard is Adobe Photoshop. Many have pre-formatted filters and special effects. Creating a file with a simple colour or gradient colour fill and printing it onto fabric is a quick-and-easy way to create pre-coloured fabrics.

BACKGROUND IMAGES

Commercially available collections of background images are available on CD-ROMs or DVDs and are usually pre-sized ready to print for desktop printers. Most are copyright or royalty free. 'Copyright free' means that the images can be used in an unrestricted way. 'Royalty free' does not mean that images are copyright free, but that you do not have to pay a royalty fee; however, you should be aware of possibly infringing copyright. Some copyrights may need to be acknowledged and may only be used for non-commercial purposes. Do read the terms and conditions on each disk. You will find that the same rules generally apply to the use of rubber stamps.

TRANSFER DYES

Transfer dyes can be purchased in powder form and as pre-mixed solutions. If you mix too much, leave the liquid to dry out in a pot to be saved and redissolved at a later date.

The term 'dye' is misleading, as transfer dyes do not work in the same way as dip dyes. The transfer-dye solution has to be painted onto paper, left to dry and offset onto fabric with a hot iron. The dye transfers (or sublimates) with heat. Many modern patterned fabrics are commercially printed in this way.

HOT-WATER ACID DYES

These dyes are used in this book only with Evolon, as the polyamide (nylon) content of the fabric will accept hot-water acid dyes. The acid in this process is vinegar or citric acid. In order for acid dyes to work effectively, the dye bath must be a minimum of 60°C (140°F), hence the technique is not suitable for all fabrics.

PAINTS

All of the paints used in this book are water-based, although not all are acrylic-based. Once dry and cured for a few hours, acrylic paints will not redissolve in water. Any water-based paint can be used on fabric without affecting the stability of the fibres.

ACRYLIC MEDIUMS

All acrylic mediums and gels manufactured for artists are polymers or copolymers and vary only in viscosity or finish. They are specifically manufactured as extenders for acrylic paints and any instructions on containers are to that end. When using them on fabric, there are two main points to consider: first, they are inert substances that will not react with fibres; second, all acrylic mediums when dry will return to their water-resistant state and will leave a stiff residue in fabric. Matt forms of gels and mediums contain matting agents and will give a more translucent finish.

PRINTING AIDS

Many printing aids on the market are acrylic-based (see above) and have been developed and promoted as digital printing aids for use on unusual surfaces such as clay or metal. Issues for textile artists are slightly different. Printing onto fabric is not in itself an issue, but hydrophobic fabrics such as Lutradur cannot absorb ink and dye-based inkjet-printed images will fade on drying. An acrylic-based printing aid alleviates this problem but leaves a stiff residue. Print.Ability is a medium that coats the fibres of fabric and holds the dye-based ink in the medium while the ink dries but does not leave a stiff residue in the fabric.

Black cartridge inks usually contain a more permanent ink. If your printer uses pigment-based inks, printing aids are not usually required.

DYE-BASED SPRAYS

The dye-based sprays used in this book are either a plain flat colour or mixed with mica powders for added lustre. Good ones should also contain a fixative, so that the mica powder or other additives will adhere to the surface of the fabric. Again, a printing aid such as Print.Ability will be required on most of the fabrics used in this book as the dye will become pale when dry if the fibres have not been able to absorb the liquid. Samples in this book use Aqua Regia, Aqua Spectrum and Aqua Fortis, which work well on fabrics.

THREADS

Without getting overly complicated, threads that will melt include polyester and polycotton sewing thread, metallic threads made from synthetic fibres (or mixtures) and nylon filaments. Threads that will not melt include cotton, silk, viscose/rayon, wool and any other natural fibre.

FOILS

Transfer foils have been developed to create a high metallic shine on paper and card and need an adhesive or a sticky glue such as Bondaweb to fix the foil to fabric. The shiny foil is manufactured on a clear carrier sheet but contains no real metal.

HOT FOILS

These are similar to transfer foils but have a tiny amount of adhesive incorporated into the foil (although there is not enough to use independently of adhesive on most fabrics, with the exception of Evolon, see page 76). Hot foils are manufactured to withstand heat up to 110ºC (230ºF) – within the range of a domestic iron.

HEALTH AND SAFETY

• Polyester, polyamide, and polypropylene are not known to produce toxic fumes when heated, but it is always advisable to work in a well-ventilated room and to wear a suitable mask if sensitive to the fumes. Prolonged exposure to these fumes may well trigger a sensitivity.

• Solvents should only be used in well-ventilated areas.

• Heat tools and soldering irons should not be left unattended when on.

USING COLOUR

Many people believe that they have no instinct for colour, but often they simply lack confidence. Learning a few basic principles of colour theory will give you a good head start. The following illustrations are examples of how to work with and combine colour.

Black and white

'Less is more' may be an overused phrase, but it is nevertheless a good principle to follow, as too many colours in a single piece of work can create a confused effect.

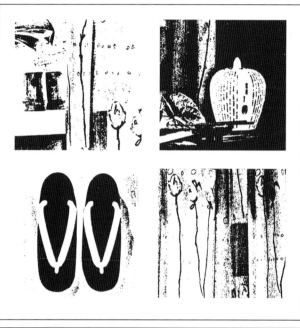

ABOVE LEFT AND LEFT: In addition to providing a lot of contrast, black-and-white images can also be used to make the image jump forwards. Gradients of colour extend the visual possibilities.

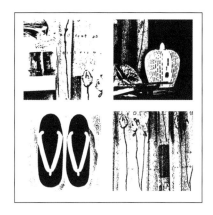
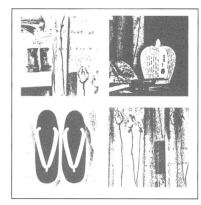
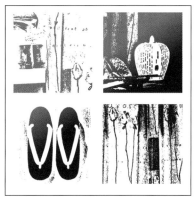

RIGHT: Each illustration uses two colours, purple and white, but further variation is achieved by using colour gradients.

One colour with white

Using just one colour against a white background removes any angst for the less-confident colour user. Not very exciting, I hear you say – but by mixing white or an extender into fabric paint or ink, you can create some wonderfully varying colour tones.

RIGHT: Again, only two colours are used in these illustrations – this time purple and black. Note how the black adds a different dimension to the artwork in comparison to the white, shown above.

One colour with black

You may think that using one (paler) colour on a black background may achieve the same as using white, but not necessarily. Your paint or ink may not be opaque and the printed image will not be reflected in as much contrast to its background. Also, mixing black into your chosen colour will alter the colour hue as black paint is usually a very dark brown or blue. Working with black as a colour needs patience, but good results can be achieved with practice. Alternatively, you could use a black image on a coloured background.

Using two colours

Combining just two colours can give mixed results and the trick here is to begin with complementary colours. There's no need to get bogged down with colour theory, but complementary colours are ones that lie opposite each other on a colour wheel; keeping a colour wheel to hand is a quick way to pick out colour combinations that should work together.

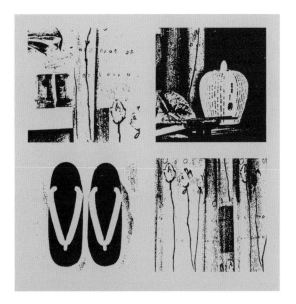
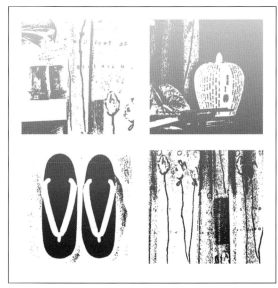
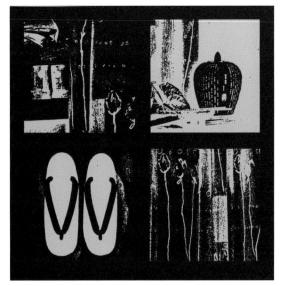

ABOVE: Purple and yellow are the two complementary colours used here, but as soon as black or white is introduced into the mix the combinations increase exponentially.

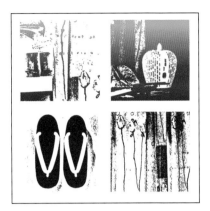 

RIGHT: Use of analogous colours creates a calming effect, while the addition of white keeps the overall effect constrained.

Using analogous colours

Analogous colours sit alongside each other on a colour wheel – blue and violet or blue and green, for example. For the purposes of constructing a workable colour scheme, two or three colours can be used – and not just as individual colours, but as a continuous colour change.

RIGHT: Again, analogous colours are used but combined with black instead of white. In this combination, the overall effect is calmer.

Multi-coloured backgrounds

Backgrounds may be a full-colour image or a commercially printed patterned fabric on which you can overprint quite successfully by using a single-colour image – particularly black on a brightly coloured background and white on a dark-coloured background.

All of the examples shown above used a very restricted colour palette and are only a small selection of possible combinations. By being disciplined in your colour choices you remove a lot of the distractions that may prevent the successful completion of the piece. Another aspect of creating a successful piece of work is varying the choice of size and scale (see pages 66–67).

Transparency

Don't forget that working with lightweight spunbonded fabrics can offer another dimension – that of transparency to give dimension and depth to an image. An extension of colour mixing is to mix colours using transparent layers rather than on a single plane.

LEFT: Samples have been placed on different-coloured fabrics to demonstrate how a translucent fabric can be altered dramatically depending upon the colour underneath. Here, transparent polyester organzas have been placed over the top of stamped and printed fabric to demonstrate the same kind of effect.

RIGHT: Rather than applying colour from an inkjet printer, this sample was painted with a water-based metallic paint and left to dry before overprinting through an inkjet printer with a black-and-white image. Transparent layers of organza create colour variation as well as depth. 30 x 20cm (12 x 8in)

COLOURING AND DYEING TECHNIQUES

Although Evolon contains a percentage of polyamide (nylon) that will accept hot-water acid dye, most spunbonded fabrics are manufactured from polyester, polyester mixes or other synthetics, so they can only be dyed in the manufacturing process and cannot subsequently be dip dyed. However, there are a number of way of applying colour to the surface.

Colouring with water-based paint

Any water-based paint can be applied to the surface of spunbonded fabrics: although a paint that has body, such as a heavy-body acrylic, is more effective in creating an opaque finish, diluted water-based paints will create a more translucent finish. When acrylic paint has dried and air cured for approximately 18–24 hours, the paint will be fixed to the surface of the

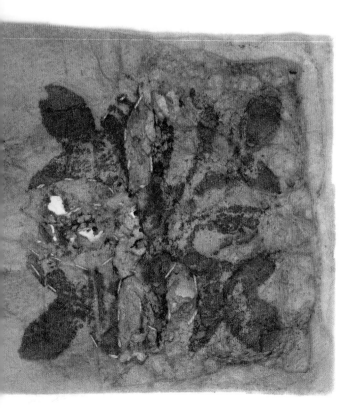

fabric and will not redissolve in water, while paint such as watercolour has little or no body and therefore will leave little residual colour. Do not leave wet fabrics to dry on paper, as the paper will over-absorb the paint and remove some or most of the colour from the surface of the fabric.

Colouring with fabric paints

If fabric paints are used, the binder contained within the paint can be heat set with an iron and will achieve a more opaque colour finish.

Colouring with dye-based sprays

These can be sprayed on randomly as desired for decorative, non-permanent effects or used in conjunction with Print.Ability as a medium to help hold the ink as it dries (as with inkjet inks).

BELOW: Each of the 230gsm Lutradur samples below has been coloured variously with acrylic paint, walnut ink and dye-based sprays. Heat distressing has caused the very heavy Lutradur to peel away as it is heated. 5 x 5cm (2 x 2in)

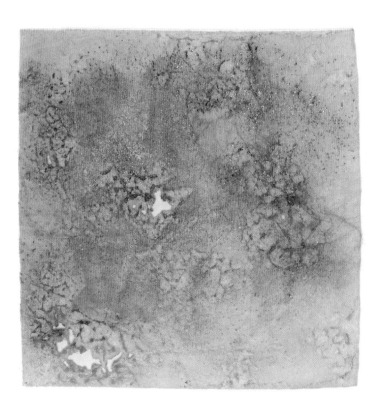
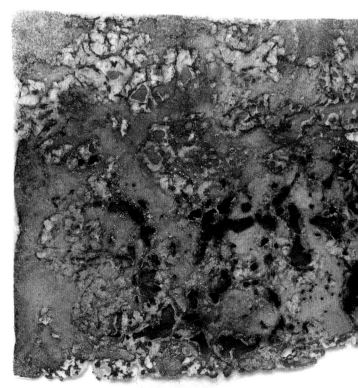

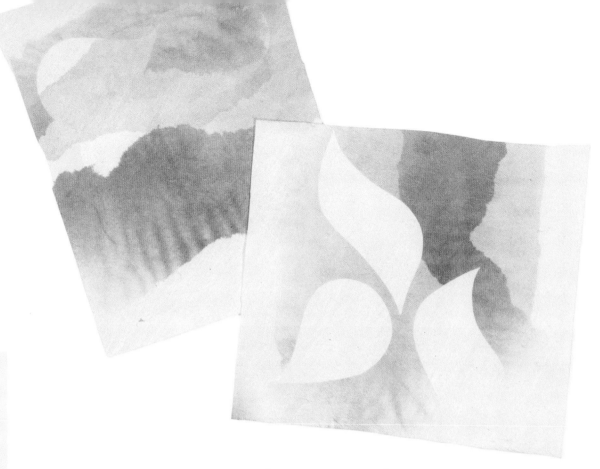

Colouring with transfer (sublimation) dyes

The most effective way of getting a good depth of colour on polyester spunbonded fabrics is to apply transfer (sublimation) dyes to the surface. The term 'dye' is potentially misleading, as transfer dyes are used in quite a different way to normal dyes. Transfer dyes are activated by heat. As heat opens up the structure of the fibre, the dye sublimates (goes from solid to gas) and is locked into the fibre as it cools. Transfer dyes can be used with any synthetic fibre as long as it can withstand high temperatures – nappy liner is not suitable.

Transfer dyes are quite straightforward to use. They can be bought either in powder form and mixed with water to form a solution or as pre-dissolved dyes. They have been available as crayons but these are no longer available in the EU. The most common method of applying transfer dyes is to paint the dye solution onto a sheet of plain paper or specialist transfer paper and allow the dye to dry. This sheet is then placed face down on the fabric surface and ironed from the back with a hot iron. Take care to prevent the bare metal of the sole of the iron coming into direct contact with any synthetic fabric, as the heat required to sublimate the dye will be much higher than the fabric can tolerate.

Transfer dyes can produce very clear results when printed onto synthetic fabrics. Variations result if the dye has been mixed to different strengths or painted on unevenly, or if the heat or pressure is not high enough or the iron has not been held in place for long enough. For this reason, better results will be obtained if a laundry press can be used. If this is not possible, a dry iron is preferable to a steam iron, as the steam vents on the plate of the iron can cause small circles to appear on the cloth if you linger too long in one place.

ABOVE LEFT: Transfer dye is prone to 'gassing', or migration of the dye particles (see the ripple effect at the bottom-left corner). This is caused by some of the dye moving around under heat and pressure, and is evident when dyes form lines or ripples of colour on the cloth.
12 x 16cm (4¾ x 6¼in)

ABOVE RIGHT: To achieve a random mixed colour, tear strips of paper painted with transfer dye and apply randomly across the fabric surface, using the plain paper shapes to mask areas.
12 x 16cm (4¾ x 6¼in)

The chart on page 124 shows which fabric are more or less suitable for transfer dyes – not because they won't work, but because the heat of the iron may be too much for fabrics such as low-temperature-melt nappy liner, as you need to linger for about 20–30 seconds to get a good, sharp, transferred image.

Stencil (mask) printing

One of the simplest methods of colouring or patterning spunbonded fabric with transfer dyes is to create a stencil, or mask, using paper shapes. Cut, punch, or tear shapes from the plain paper and place them on your fabric surface. Using freezer paper is helpful, as you can iron the shapes in place before printing. Take a piece or pieces of dye-painted paper, place them over the top of the shapes, and offset the transfer dyes in the normal way. When the fabric is cool again, peel away your shapes. By taking two or more different colours of painted transfer-dye papers, tearing or cutting them into strips, and randomly offsetting the dye, you can create many colour mixes and build a denser coloration.

BELOW: Try to remember that shapes can be created by negative space (the white areas left behind). In this sample, four strips of paper were laid onto Lutradur and transfer dye offset over the top.

15 x 12cm (6 x 4¾in)

Creating text 'images' using transfer dyes

Text 'images' can be transferred to any fabric surface using a laser printer. Print out your text (in reverse) and paint some transfer dye over the printed pages. You will notice that the water-based liquid beads up on areas of toner. When the dye paper is dry, offset the colour with heat in the normal way. If your heat source is very hot, some of the loose toner will transfer, but after the first print or two, the toner will have been fixed and you will produce perfect negative imprints. The print sheets can be re-coated several times before they become too saturated with dye to work properly.

ABOVE: Negative space is used to create the above image. Here a laser-printed photocopy was painted with transfer dye and used to heat-transfer the negative image onto fabric.
15 x 12cm (6 x 4¾in)

Inkjet printing

Any of the spunbonded fabrics can be inkjet printed and the technique is described in detail on pages 31–37. This is one of the simplest ways of applying colour to cloth but the results will vary depending on the absorbency and density of the fibre.

Colouring with oil pastels and paintsticks

Unlike paints and other wet media, oil pastels and Markal Paintstiks can be applied directly onto the surface of the fabric with a drawing or rubbing action. The deposited colour can then be rubbed in with other colours to obtain a graduated effect. If further mixing or thinning is required, add a small amount of thinner or white spirit to the surface and brush it into the pastel to obtain a more translucent effect.

Note: If you are using oil-based pastels with thinners, be aware that the solvent could immediately, or with time, dissolve the synthetic fibres of the spunbonded fabric.

Hot-water acid dyes

In normal circumstances, most synthetic fibres have to be dyed during the manufacturing process; they cannot subsequently be dip dyed. This is true of most spunbonded fabrics, with the exception of Evolon, which is a mixture of polyester and polyamide (nylon). Nylon was one of the first synthetic fabrics to be produced and, because it has a different chemical structure to polyester, it can be dip dyed with hot-water acid dyes. In fact, you can obtain acid dyes specially formulated for dyeing nylon although this is not necessary for home dyeing.

Prepare your dye bath and dye as you would to dye wool or silk, mixing a small quantity of dye following the manufacturer's instructions. The 'acid' in acid dyeing is merely vinegar or citric acid and the temperature range for dyeing is 60–90ºC (140–194ºF). Try to stay at the lower end of the temperature range, as any creases that form in the synthetic fibres will be hard to remove. Evolon can be successfully dyed at 60ºC (140ºF).

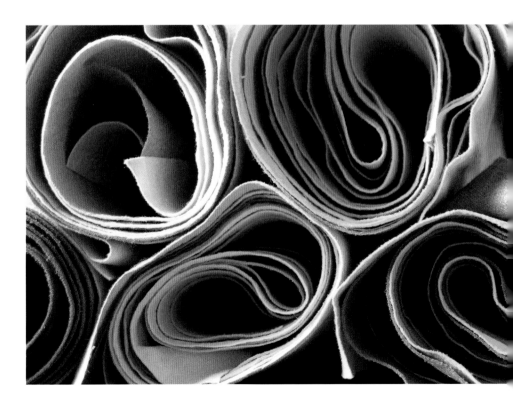

RIGHT: Because Evolon contains only a small percentage of dyeable fibre, the resulting colour will always be a soft tone rather than a strong, bright colour.

CREATING TEXTURE

Different spunbonded fabrics react to different heat-distressing techniques but, as a general guide, nappy liner will distress most readily, Evolon will require a concentrated effort, and most of the polyester-fibre fabrics will be somewhere in between.

Lace effects

Spunbonded and other synthetic fabrics respond readily to heat distressing with a heat gun. If the heat gun is placed close to the fabric during heating, holes will form readily in the fabric structure; however, for a more even effect, hold the heat gun away from the surface and waft it backwards and forwards until the desired effect is achieved. In order to keep the fabric flat, place it in a fairly large embroidery hoop while heating takes place. Keep moving the hoop along if you are distressing a large piece of fabric.

When heat distressing any spunbonded fabric in a free style (simply passing the heat gun across the surface of the fabric), make sure there is enough space behind the fabric for the lacy holes to appear. If, for example, fabric is stretched in an embroiderery hoop placed firm against a hard, flat surface, the holes will not form readily. Creating an evenly spaced series of holes takes a little practice and is only achieved once you have built up a smooth rhythm of moving the heat gun across the surface of the fabric. All spunbonded fabrics melt more easily if they have not been painted.

Evolon has the same random structure as Lutradur, but is a mix of polyamide and polyester which has been textured in the manufacturing process and results in a softer, more opaque structure. It has a slightly higher melting point than pure polyester fabrics, so it requires a little more effort to get a distressed effect.

Using a stencil when heat distressing

If you want to protect parts of the fabric and prevent them from being heat distressed, apply paint or another medium to selected areas using a patterning device such as a foam stamp or stencil. You can then apply heat to the surface, either while the medium is still wet or when it has dried. Either way, the paint will provide a mask and the heat distressing will mostly take effect only on unpainted areas of fabric.

3D expanding medium can also be used as a mask. You must consider beforehand how much you want the medium to expand, as a small amount will expand far more than expected. To counter this effect, leave the 3D expanding medium to dry before you apply heat. 3D expanding medium can also be pre-mixed with acrylic paints to create a coloured pattern, which will also expand less when heated.

Another technique is to pre-bond a natural fabric to the surface of Lutradur (or other spunbonded material) with Bondaweb; this, too, will act as a mask.

RIGHT: This detail of a bodice from a dress (see page 51) illustrates perfectly how Lutradur distresses with heat.

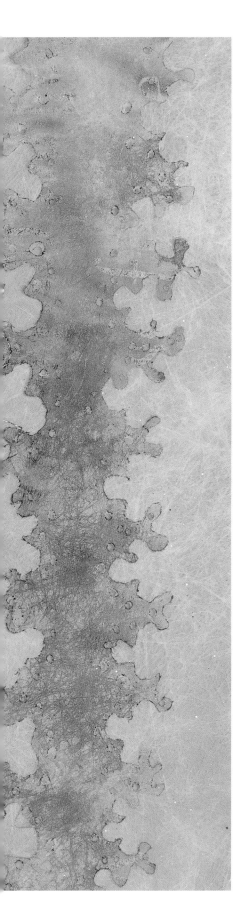

Cutting with a soldering iron

All spunbonded textiles can be cut very easily with a soldering iron, but Evolon requires a smoother, slower action, taking a little more effort. Make sure that the soldering iron is up to temperature, as this will make the cutting action easier. Hold and use the soldering iron in the same way as a pen to cut the fabric.

If the fabric has been painted or dyed beforehand, cutting out shapes or shaping edges will leave a tidemark effect around the soldered edge. This gives an intensified colouration and makes the soldered edges slightly fatter, resulting in a raised profile. This effect is not particularly visible to the naked eye; however, it can be employed to great effect as it will pick up small amounts of hot foils without any adhesive.

Welding layers with a soldering iron

If one layer of fabric is placed on top of another as it is cut, the two layers will weld together enough to keep them stable for any overstitching or other effects to be employed. Different synthetic fabrics can be welded together to achieve pleasing effects – for example, welding polyester organza to Evolon (see the lower sample on page 81).

Applying transfer (hot) foils

The thermoplastic nature of the fibres used in spunbonded textiles means that they will heat and melt just enough to form a bond with transfer foil, using a domestic iron. Transfer foils usually need a bonding agent, but in this case, just place the transfer foil shiny side uppermost and apply the heat from an iron. Note that placing paper between the iron and the foil dissipates the heat too much, which makes it difficult to achieve the required combination of heat and pressure. The slightly raised, soldered edges of the Lutradur will take a transfer foil quite easily as described above.

Note: Hot transfer foils were developed to be used at a temperature of around 110ºC (230ºF), which is well within the range of a domestic iron. If the iron is too hot the foil will become dull and will resist being reused or even being lifted by tacky glues. If hot foil is used at the correct temperature, not only will you get consistently successful results, but the carrier sheet will not melt when placed directly into contact with the foot plate of a domestic iron. You need to be brave with this, but it does work.

LEFT: Lutradur will cut easily and smoothly with a soldering iron. Here, dyed and printed 30gsm Lutradur has been cut into narrow strips and stitched onto additional layers of Lutradur and brightly coloured foam.

Layering

Using several layers of synthetic fibres that have been fused together can create dimension and give an optical illusion of depth. Layers are also a good way to build colour, enhance colour or emphasize an area of colour. Similarly, developing small areas of additional texture creates contrast within an overall textured surface.

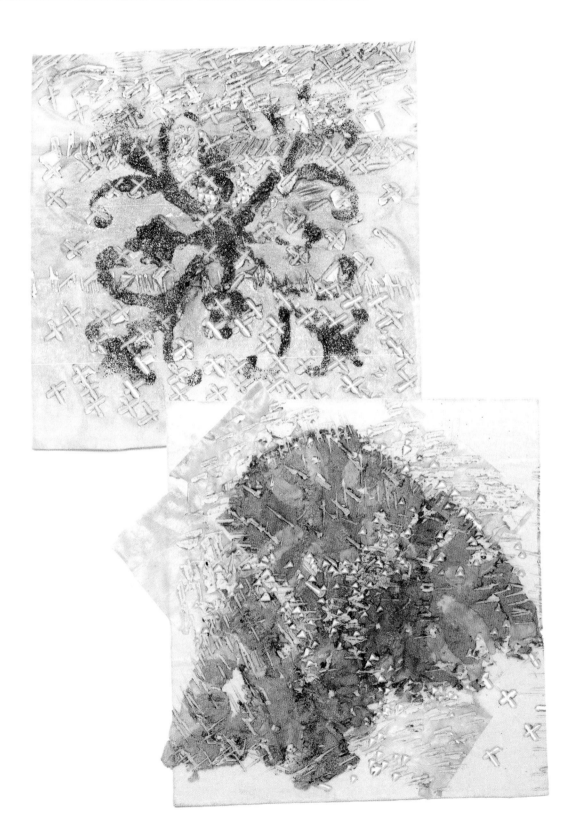

USING IMAGES

The choice of an image is a personal one but, from a technical point of view, a contrasting black-and-white image will produce the clearest results, particularly if printed on a slightly textured surface or on translucent fabrics. Full-colour images will prove the most challenging as fine detail can be lost. Anything in between these two options can be experimented with to acheive the effect you are looking for.

Inkjet printing

First, you need to be clear about the difference between an inkjet printer and a laser printer. The term 'photocopier' is often misapplied to desktop scanner/printers/copiers, which use inks, whereas an office photocopier uses toner, which is a type of powdered plastic that is heat set at quite high temperatures. This is not a problem for printing onto paper, but could prove disastrous for heat-sensitive fabrics such as Lutradur (and your laser printer).

Desktop inkjet printers are developing continually; basic and older printers tend to use dye-based inks, and newer, better-quality inkjet printers use pigment-based inks. Printers that use more than two ink cartridges probably contain pigment-based ink, as well as the inks that claim to be fade proof. You need to establish which kind of ink your printer uses. A simple test is to print an image onto paper and, once it is dry, place it in water. If the ink runs readily, it is dye-based; if it does not run, it is probably pigment-based. The most important point to note here is whether or not it will run and then you can adjust to your working methods accordingly.

Both dye- and pigment-based inks will print onto spunbonded fabrics. Pigment-based inks appear to give a better image initially but, particularly on Lutradur, the image can bleed or fade over time. Consider using a printing aid (see page 35) to mitigate this.

Printing fabric through an inkjet printer is simplicity itself. Most smooth-surfaced fabrics will pass though a desktop printer. Lutradur (70gsm or heavier), will pass through unaided, while others need to be stabilized on backing paper. The oddly named 'freezer paper' is a paper with a silicone coating on one side that is ironed onto the back of the fabric to act as a carrier sheet. Heat-activated adhesive paper will do the same job and is much cheaper.

LEFT: On both samples, a layer of heat-distressable tissue has been placed over 230gsm Lutradur and cut with a soldering iron. The heat has cut through both layers to the Lutradur below, creating a sculpted surface texture.
12 x 12cm (4¾ x 4¾in)

Selecting an image for printing

If you are going to scan an image into your computer and this image is not your own, be mindful of copyright (see page 11). If you are working with greyscale or colour images, scan them in at a resolution of 300ppi so that you can alter the size of the image without it degrading too much. Line drawings should be scanned in at 600ppi. If you are taking photographs for use in textile work, ensure that your camera setting is on a resolution of 300ppi whenever possible.

There are no hard rules about which images work best on fabric, but these are my tips:
- Black-and-white (only) images work best due to the high contrast. Black-and-white images printed onto pre-dyed or coloured fabric work very well.
- Greyscale images work well on single-colour or simple backgrounds.
- Full-colour images will only produce a sharp image on a white background with a smooth surface.

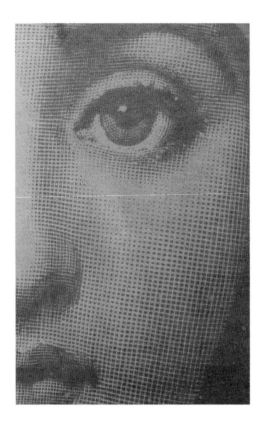

ABOVE: In this piece, Evolon has been dyed yellow and then overdyed with red in small areas to create an ombre effect. A black-and-white image has then been inkjet printed over the top.
25 x 22cm (10 x 8⅝in)

ABOVE: Evolon in this piece was dyed turquoise and then printed with a black-and-white image to create the background. Polyester organza was then placed in an embroidery hoop to keep it taut and then placed on top of the Evolon. The hoop enables the surface of the organza to stay in contact with the surface of the Evolon and to prevent it from clinging to the tip of the soldering iron. The sandal shapes were then cut out through the organza with the soldering iron and at the same time fused to the Evolon background.
25 x 21cm (10 x 8¼in)

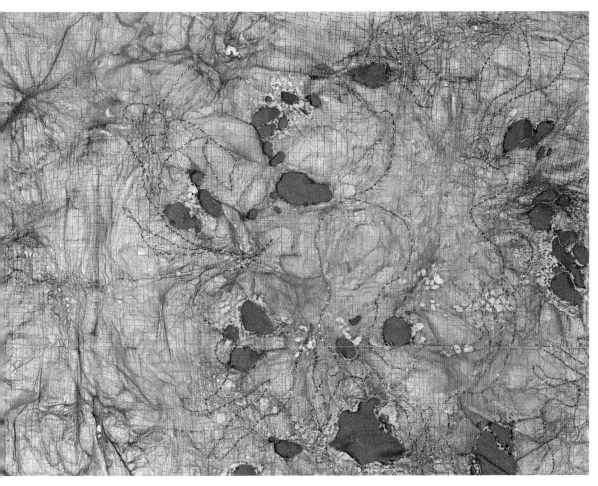

LEFT AND BELOW: These Tyvek samples were printed with an inkjet printer using a gradient colour fill. Tyvek, like most synthetic fabrics, is hydrophobic and therefore water-based inks do not naturally absorb, although coating the printing surface with Print.Ability helps the ink to adhere to the surface. The samples were subsequently distressed with a heat gun and then stitched over a brightly coloured back cloth. For the Tyvek to remain flat when being heat distressed, the sample shown below was placed in an embroidery hoop during heat distressing. 29 x 21cm (11½ x 8¼in)

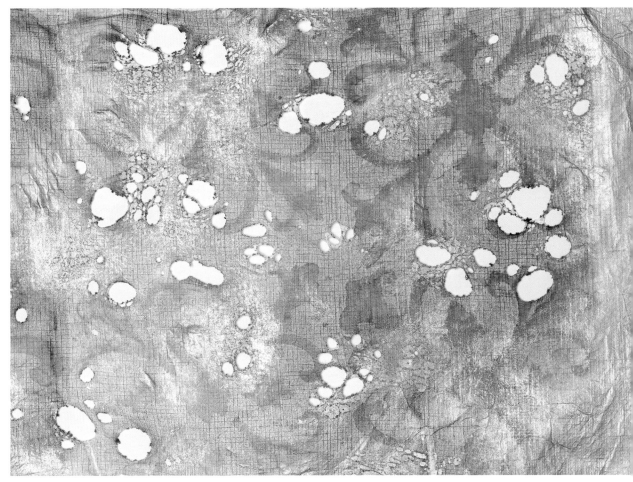

Preparing fabric for a desktop printer

A few basic preparations will ensure that fabrics can be printed quickly and easily using a desktop printer.

- Prepare your fabric to standard paper measurements, such as A4 or US Letter. Make sure your piece of fabric is cut square.
- Place your fabric on the freezer paper and adhere with an iron. Ensure that there are no air bubbles in the supporting paper sheet.
- Turn about 1cm (³/₈in) of paper back over the leading edge and if necessary stick a strip of masking tape along the rear of the top edge to strengthen and stabilize it.
- Snip both corners of the leading edge to a 45 degree angle.
- Place the fabric in the printer tray and print as normal.
- If the fabric jams in the printer during printing, press the eject button. If this does not work, switch off your printer and gently pull the fabric through to release it. Some printers have a lever to increase or decrease the pressure of the internal rollers.
- Each printer has its own eccentricities, but most inkjet printers will print smooth-surfaced fabrics.

BELOW: This sample demonstrates how inkjet images can be created on heat-distressable tissue by using the printing aid Print.Ability to stabilize the ink.
12 x 12cm (4¾ x 4¾in)

Printing aids

Pure polyester fibres are hydrophobic, so when they are printed through an inkjet printer, the ink will be laid on the surface of the fibre but cannot be absorbed. So as the ink dries, the image will become paler and paler. Evolon, as a next-generation fibre, is texturized, which makes it absorbent. The problem in this case, though, is that the fabric is over-absorbent and an inkjet-printed image can bleed with time as the print dries. This can be counteracted by adjusting the amount of ink that is printed onto the surface – but this can result in a paler image.

Pre-treating fabric with Print.Ability before printing will correct both these problems. Print.Ability holds the ink on the fabric surface and allows it to dry, regardless of the fabric type or construction. Most importantly of all, it will not leave any stiff residue in the fabric. The samples shown below show print tests carried out on Lutradur and Evolon.

Most of the other popular mediums on the market manufactured for this purpose are usually a form of acrylic polymer and will leave a stiff handle in fabric. Some are transparent and some are white or opaque, but all have been developed to accept printed and other inks.

ABOVE: Lutradur with Print.Ability, not rinsed in water (top left); with Print.Ability, rinsed in water (bottom left); no print aid, not rinsed in water (top right) and no print aid, rinsed in water (bottom right).

ABOVE: Evolon with Print.Ability, not rinsed in water (top left); with Print.Ability, rinsed in water (bottom left); no print aid, not rinsed in water (top right) and no print aid, rinsed in water (bottom right).

Creative techniques using Print.Ability

Using a foam stamp, print areas of fabric with Print.Ability and leave to dry. You are working fairly blind here unless you colour the Print.Ability with an additive such as dilute acrylic paint, mica powder or some other effect. When the Print.Ability is dry, spritz with dye-based sprays and leave to dry. Plunge the dry fabric into cool water to discharge any loose dye. (Remember that loose dye in the water will back-stain the fabric to some extent; the addition of a scourer such as Colsperse or Synthrapol will help to prevent this.) The colour will remain where you have stamped the fabric with Print.Ability. Try the same process using a stencil to achieve similar effects.

ABOVE: Print.Ability was painted onto the surface of a foam stamp, stamped on heavyweight paper Tyvek, and left to dry. The surface was then spritzed with dye-based sprays and dried again. The discharge effect was created by placing the piece in water to discharge the loose dye from the background. Hot foils were then printed off randomly across the surface with an iron. 10 x 10cm (4 x 4in)

Inkjet print and discharge

This piece of 230gsm Lutradur has been stamped with Print.Ability in the same way as the book shown opposite. Additional dye-based spray was applied to the surface to intensify the colour.

10 x 15cm (4 x 6in)

Print.Ability will prevent your inkjet-printed images from discharging into water. Using the same principle, create your stamped image using Print.Ability – but instead of spritzing with dye-based sprays to colour the fabric, overprint a solid or gradient colour over the surface using an inkjet printer. When dry, discharge your fabric by gently rinsing it in water with a scourer (Colsperse). This technique usually produces very crisp results.

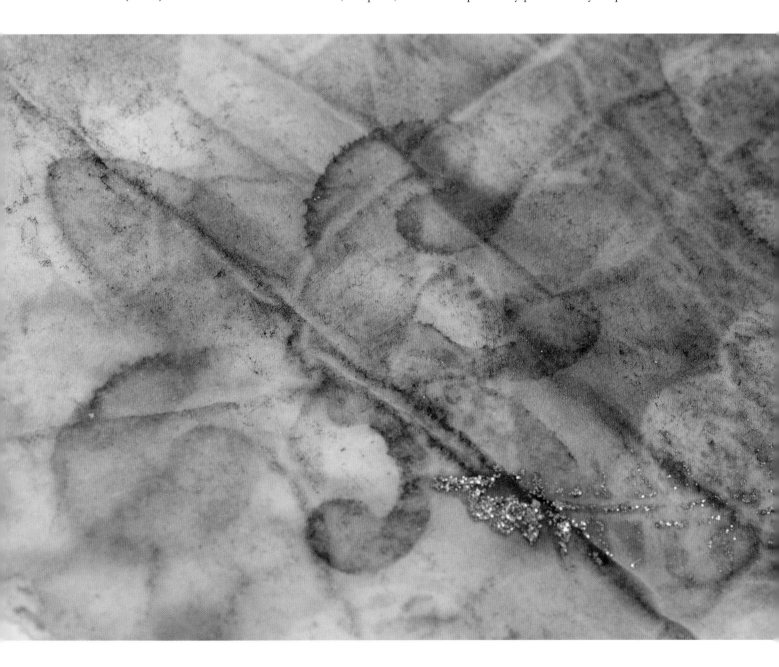

Toner transfer printing

Spunbonded fabrics are almost always constructed from synthetic fibres, which are particularly well suited to receiving images or text in the form of toner from a photocopied or laser-printed image. Toner is essentially a powdered plastic that is set by heat in the printer and can be reheated to some extent and pressed onto a fabric surface. Black-and-white images or text work best, and each printer uses different forms of toner, but essentially if you place a bold, printed image face down on the fabric surface and press from the back with a hot iron, the toner will remelt and stick, as synthetic fibres stick more easily to melted toner. The results can be a little uncertain but the technique is well worth trying.

RIGHT: An image of St Paul's Cathedral was photocopied then transferred to the Evolon by using a hot iron to melt the toner from the back of the copy. Polyester organza was then laid over the top of the image and soldered around the edge of the outline of the building.
22 x 30cm (8⅝ x 12in)

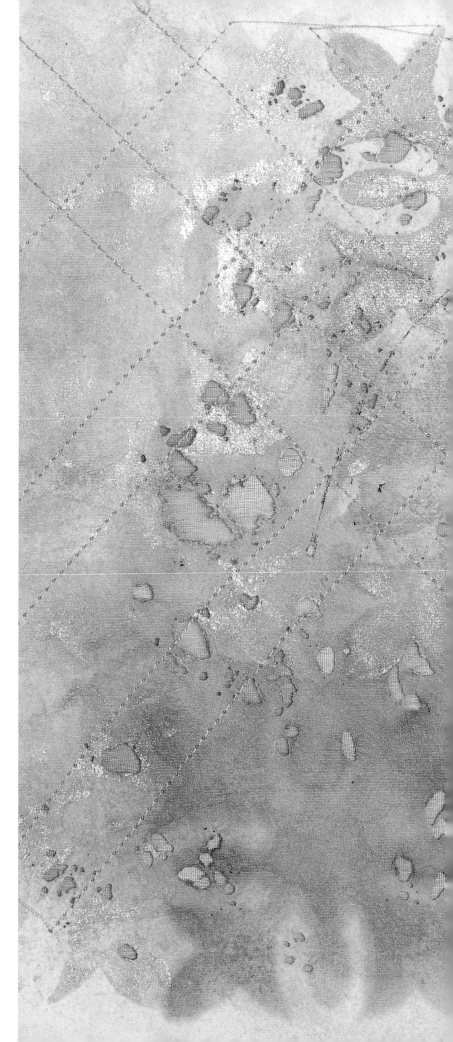

Stencilling and block printing

All spunbonded fabrics can be printed in more traditional ways such as screen printing, block printing and stencil prints. Investigate the availability of stencils, particularly those produced for interior decoration – although they are expensive, there are some unusual images available in various sizes and scales. Alternatively, try cutting your own foam stamps using a crafting tool. Lots of possibilities lie in unexpected places.

Ink pads

Water-based ink pads come in two basic types – dye-based and pigment-based. You need to familiarize yourself with the differences and apply your knowledge accordingly. Generally, dye-based inks will discharge in water, and pigment-based ones will not – much the kind of results you may get with desktop inkjet printers. Rather surprisingly, even very detailed rubber stamps will render fine detail on fabrics like Evolon.

Solvent-based ink pads can be used on synthetic spunbonded fabrics for permanent colour, with the caveat that the solvent may eat into the synthetic fibres with time.

To apply colour directly from an ink pad onto fabric, simply drag the face of the ink pad across the surface of the fabric for a distressed, uneven effect. Alternatively, apply images with a rubber stamp in the traditional way. Ink-pad re-inkers can be used in the same way as regular inks; paint or spray them onto the surface of the fabric.

LEFT: A foam stamp loaded with a diluted solution of acrylic paint was printed onto crystal spunbonded fabric. After heat distressing, the crisp, textured surface was hand stitched onto a backing of undyed Evolon Soft.

FABRICS

Spunbonded, industrial fabrics are the biggest trend in creative textiles, offering possibilities never seen before in terms of both novel construction and unique deconstruction techniques. As new developments are made, so a new use will be found for them.

LUTRADUR

Lutradur is the most popular of the spunbonded synthetic fabrics available and is manufactured in different weights. It was developed primarily for use as an industrial fabric – for example, as a carpet backing particularly for the automotive industry – so you probably have Lutradur all around you when you are out in your car. It is made from 100 per cent polyester spun fibres that are thermally bonded and has a flat, calendered surface.

The lightest weight of Lutradur (30gsm) works well combined with fine fabrics such as organza. It is quite translucent, so when any piece of work is mounted on top of another coloured fabric, the overall colour scheme is altered, sometimes giving the same effect as shot fabric. Colouring it first will provide some depth of colour or colour mixing, although 30gsm Lutradur is not dense enough to give a deep colour.

Mediumweight Lutradur (70gsm) is the most versatile of all weights available, as it is strong enough to give physical support yet dense enough to reflect additional colour where required without being too heavy. It is also fine enough to be heat distressed without producing an excessively dense fabric. This weight is also available in black – technically charcoal in colour.

Heavier weights of Lutradur (100 and 130gsm) are more densely formed, reasonably self supporting and are ideal for constructing free-standing objects such as books or smaller three-dimensional objects. They can be fed through an inkjet printer without having to be stabilized on freezer paper.

Lutradur XL (230gsm) is a much denser, opaque fabric that, when heat-distressed, appears to melt away in layers. Lutradur XL is also thick enough to create a sculpted surface using a soldering iron.

With the success of Lutradur in recent years, the introduction of new weights is planned including 18gsm, 50gsm and 300gsm. 18gsm is a very fine, softer version of Lutradur, 50gsm bridges the gap between 30 and 70gsm, while 300gsm is similar to a felt and is constructed by a needle-felting process rather than thermal bonding.

RIGHT: Two Lutradur weights were used here. The upper layer, of Lutradur 30gsm, has been coloured with transfer dyes and small squares were cut out using a soldering iron. This layer was placed on top of a layer of Lutradur XL and, by marking the surface with a soldering iron, the two layers were fused together. The cut-out squares were then stitched back onto the surface using a contrasting Perle thread.
43 x 37cm (17 x 14½in)

TECHNIQUES FOR WORKING WITH LUTRADUR

The unique selling point of Lutradur is that it is available in qualities from diaphanous to lusciously dense but always with inherent strength. It can be formed into whatever you want it to be and despite its appearance can be coloured and decorated using straightforward processes.

BELOW: Small squares of Bondaweb were pre-dyed with hot-water acid dye and fused to the surface of a painted piece of 70gsm Lutradur. Hot foil was adhered randomly to the pieces of Bondaweb. Rows of machine satin stitch complete the effect.
47 x 36cm (18½ x 14¼in)

Colouring Lutradur

The samples illustrated here have had small pieces of Bondaweb ironed to the surface, with the whole piece then being dipped into hot-water acid dye. Because heat-set adhesive fabrics such as Bondaweb can be dyed with acid dyes, the Bondaweb will absorb the dye, whereas the Lutradur, which cannot be dip dyed, will release any loose dye. As a result, you are left with dyed pieces of Bondaweb and undyed Lutradur. In practice, though, some back staining in the rinse water will slightly colour some spunbonded fabrics, so carry out tests first.

Some of the Lutradur here was then painted with transfer dye, which behaves like a watercolour treatment. The Lutradur was then ironed to set the dye, unlike the more normal technique of applying transfer dye. (For more information on colouring and dyeing techniques see pages 20–25).

Additional decoration such as lustre powder, holeless beads and foil, were added, all of which will adhere to the Bondaweb when heat is reapplied. (Futher information on applying foils is given on page 29).

ABOVE RIGHT: This sample has had foils and interference powders heat set onto the Bondaweb for extra dimension.
24 x 24cm (9½ x 9½in)

CENTRE RIGHT: Small pieces of Bondaweb, pre-dyed in hot-water acid dye, were applied to a piece of 30gsm Lutradur and painted with transfer dyes. This was stitched to a coloured foam backing, which provides both a stable base and background colour to give depth. Machine satin stitching through all the layers completes this very simply constructed piece.
24 x 24cm (9½ x 9½in)

BELOW RIGHT: Like the others on this page, this piece was constructed using transfer dyes as paint, dyed Bondaweb, hot foils, glitter and simple stitching.
24 x 24cm (9½ x 9½in)

Using colour and transparency

White Lutradur that has had colour applied to the surface can be subtly altered by being mounted on a coloured background. The translucent nature of the Lutradur will allow some of the underlying colour to show through, thus modifying the colour of the dyed Lutradur and creating some very subtle colour mixes and effects. A piece of work that looks a little disappointing on its own can be transformed by placing it over the top of another colour: garish colours become subtle combinations and dull, lifeless ones can be lifted.

BELOW: This simple landscape piece was constructed using Bondaweb, foils, beads and simple stitching. The landscape is suggested by the overlapping of the Bondaweb but, as Lutradur is translucent, different effects can be achieved by placing different, stronger-coloured fabrics underneath.

42 x 25cm (16½ x 10in)

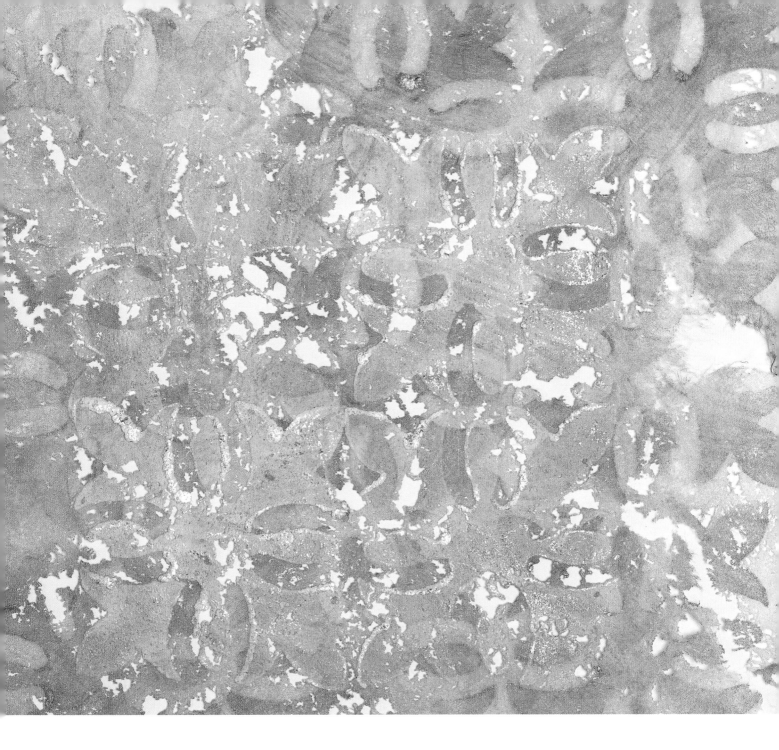

Using masks with Lutradur

ABOVE: Many of the pieces of Lutradur in this book have used one of two or three different foam stamps. This example shows how one stamp used in different combinations of colour and medium can vary the final effect. 20 x 20cm (8 x 8in)

One of the best patterning techniques for Lutradur and other spunbonded fabrics is to use a mask. Most fabric paints, acrylic paints, 3D expanding mediums – indeed, anything that has some body to it – will act as a mask on the surface of Lutradur when a heat source is applied. The fabric will only melt or distress where it is left exposed. The paint or medium will keep the underlying fabric reasonably flat and will take additional embellishing such as more paint, gilding waxes or adhesives.

Distressing Lutradur

Despite its inherent strength provided by its construction, distressing techniques can transform a fabric tough enough to hold concrete rubble into a breathtaking, fractured delicate surface.

Magenta dress

The bodice of the dress shown here is made of white 70gsm Lutradur, pre-coloured with transfer dyes in magenta and golden yellow, and mounted on a golden yellow fabric. Mediumweight Lutradur is still translucent enough to allow colour combining to alter the overall effect, creating a soft overall tone. Before each piece was pinned to a dress form – one to the front and one to the back – 3D expanding medium was used to stamp fleur-de-lys motifs onto the bodice. The surface was then heat distressed using a heat gun, which enabled the excess fabric to be gently moulded and shrunk to the body shape. With care most of the excess fabric, which would normally be shaped by seaming, can be eliminated by this method. The resulting fabric has a very textured surface.

The surface of the bodice has been distressed with a heat gun, and attached to the under bodice with random, cross stitches. The 'seams' were stitched, again with quite random bold stitching.

The dress skirt is made of nylon tulle, dyed with hot-water acid dyes to match the bodice. Large pieces of fabric are often best dyed in a washing machine. Hot-water acid dye requires a temperature of 60–90ºC (140–194ºF) and automatic washing machines are excellent at maintaining the correct temperature as well as keeping the fabric agitated in the dye for an even coverage. In practice, acid dyes will dye at 50–60ºC (122–140ºF), but by dyeing nylon at the higher end of the temperature range, creases will become permanent in the fabric; this is not normally desirable, but in this case it works to good effect to complete the distressed look.

RIGHT: Despite the tough appearance of Lutradur 70gsm, it is versatile enough to accept surface treatments such as colouring and heat distressing, which creates the illusion of delicacy and fragmentation.

LEFT: Close-up detail of the bodice of the dress showing the distressed Lutradur effect.

Gothic book cover

The front of the book cover shown below was made using the same basic method as the dress bodice on page 51, but in order to prevent the fabric from buckling and warping as the heat distressing was applied to the surface, the Lutradur was placed in an embroidery hoop. Because the fabric cannot warp, holes are created much more quickly. Additional surface embellishment was created by free machine stitching the fabric while it was still in the embroidery hoop, hand stitching on small iridescent beads, and enhancing the 3D expanding medium with rub-on gilding waxes.

The back cover shown right illustrates a method of using transfer (sublimation) dyes in conjuction with a laser-printed photocopy of text (printed in reverse) instead of plain paper to offset the dye in order to produce printed text on the surface. This is how the front looked before it was embellished. For more information on using transfer dyes, see page 24. The text was printed randomly across the surface, using two or three pieces of text as well as different colours. The overall deeper colour was achieved by mounting the pieces for the book cover over a layer of scarlet synthetic organza. The front and back covers were made as two separate pieces and joined by overlapping and stitching with a close satin stitch.

The book cover shown left was made using the same method to distress the surface of the Lutradur, but with the 3D expanding medium pre-coloured with blue acrylic paint.

ABOVE: Exploit the transparency of the Lutradur by placing it over coloured fabric. Here it has been placed over red organza.

OPPOSITE: An ancient, faded effect can be achieved by adding blue acrylic paint to the 3D expanding medium and placing the Lutradur onto yellow fabric.

BELOW: The front of the book can be enhanced by adding small glass beads and gold organza.

Cutting and soldering Lutradur

Because of the synthetic polyester fibres that form Lutradur, a craft soldering iron will cut through the fibres with little or no resistance. Similarly, because of the nature of Lutradur's spunbonded construction, the craft iron can be used to etch through partial thicknesses to form marks on the surface.

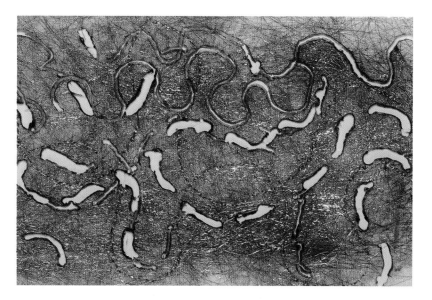

LEFT: Cutting and welding can be used not just with Lutradur but in combination with other heat-distressable fabrics – Angelina fibres are heat sensitive, too.
10 x 3cm (4 x 1¼in)

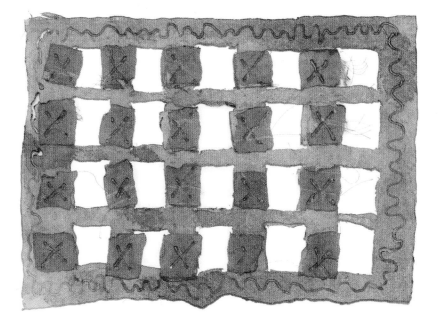

LEFT: Using a soldering iron on thick Lutradur creates surface pattern as well as dimension by cutting only partially through the material.
12 x 7cm (4¾ x 2¾in)

RIGHT: This piece is a combination of different techniques carried out on a practice piece of polyester organza on a backing of 30gsm Lutradur.
13 x 22cm (5⅛ x 8⅝in)

Solvent transfer of images and text onto Lutradur

This is an old technique, but is a wonderful way to explore the full potential of Lutradur. By its very nature this is a hit-and-miss process, but it can give some very good results. Toner has an affinity with synthetic fibres, making this technique easy to complete. Print out a piece of black text or a black-and-white image (not greyscale) via a laser printer or office photocopier, remembering to reverse any text as this is an offset process. Place the copy face down on the Lutradur and puddle a small amount of acetone or cellulose thinners onto the paper. Rub or press with a small cloth, taking care not to let the paper move. As the toner melts, it will stick to the surface of the Lutradur. Peel off the copy when the transfer is complete. Take care to work in a well-ventilated area, and use a mask when working with cellulose thinners. Always remember that solvents are flammable liquids and take necessary precautions.

RIGHT: This piece is a combination of nylon voile and small pieces of 30gsm Lutradur, both of which have had letter forms solvent transferred onto the surface; Lutradur letters were collaged onto the surface with random stitching.
50 x 32cm (19¾ x12½in)

Welding layers

If you place two or more layers of synthetic fibre such as a ply of polyester organza and fine Lutradur together, you can cut through the two layers and weld them together at the same time. Synthetic fabrics are, by their very nature, quite bouncy and will cling to your soldering iron as you try to work it, so place both layers of fabric in an embroidery hoop to clamp the two fabrics together while you solder around the shapes.

BELOW: The verse on this example was toner transferred onto a piece of 30gsm Lutradur and applied to a piece of purple organza. The letters were cut out with a soldering iron and reapplied to the surface by heat fusing.
35 x 22cm (13¾ x 8⅝in)

Shoe

Lutradur XL will struggle to pass through an inkjet printer, but it can be stamped and coloured with dye-based products such as Aqua Spectrum spritzes. Here, the Lutradur was printed with a foam stamp 'inked' with Print.Ability and allowed to dry. It was then sprayed with Aqua Spectrum dye-based spritz and again allowed to dry. The whole piece was then placed in a bowl of water. Where the dye combines with the Print.Ability, the colour remains, while the loose dye on the untreated parts of the surface discharges (these print and discharge techniques are described on pages 36–37). Distressing was achieved by applying a heat gun to the surface. Lutradur XL distresess just as quickly as any of the other weights, but if heat is applied a little more judiciously, it will dissolve in 'layers' and create a more dimensional surface.

To form the shoe, a two-piece paper pattern (one each for the front and heel sections) was made from a normal shoe and the shoe itself used as a mould to make a papier mâché last. First, the shoe was wrapped in many layers of clingfilm and then layered up with lots of small pieces of newspaper soaked in a dilute solution of PVA adhesive. Each (thin) layer was left to dry with a minimum of three layers being created. When the new 'shoe' was dry, it was pulled away from the real shoe and the clingfilm carefully removed. The surface was sanded to eliminate any lumps and bumps and the dried shoe was able to stand under its own weight. The paper pattern was then used to cut the Lutradur XL to form the shoe upper, and moulded around the papier mâché last. Once the shoe was fully formed, it was embellished and hand stitched.

RIGHT: If you are going to make more than one of anything, make them on a production line so the two items can be equally matched.
10 x 22cm (4 x 8⅝in)

Needlefelting Lutradur

Lutradur XL can be needle felted quite successfully. It is stable enough to needle felt into without any support: simply lay wool or other fibres on the surface and punch the fibres into the Lutradur with a felting needle or embellisher. Needlefelting can be applied decoratively on the front surface or worked on the back to reflect any distressing.

Additional embellishments and Aqua Regia dye-based sprays can also be used and, although the polyester fibres cannot absorb the liquid dyes, the density of the fibres will intensify any colour applied to the surface. Paints and other surface colours work well.

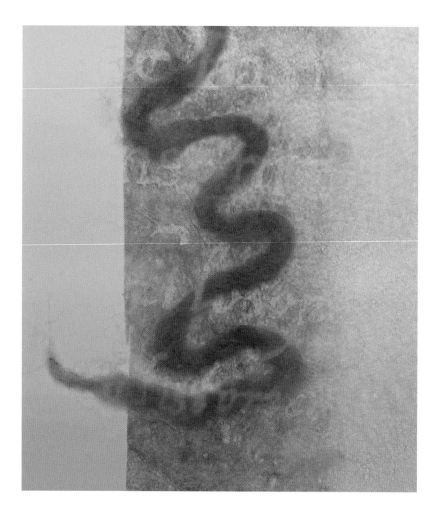

ABOVE: Even fine weights of spunbonded fabric can be needlefelted. Here, strands of bamboo fibre were needlefelted into a piece of 17gsm crystal spunbonded fabric, then a transfer dye was laid over the top.
12 x 5cm (4½ x 2in)

RIGHT: Lutradur XL has been partially heat distressed and then stitched with viscose machine thread. Lutradur XL will trap fibres that are needle felted into its surface. Here, merino fibres have been used.
20 x 28cm (7¾ x 11in)

Colouring charcoal Lutradur

Any method of colouring dark versions of Lutradur will give very
limited effects but from a starting point of charcoal rather than black,
unusual illusions can be created – much like backlighting a fabric. The best
approach here is to work the effects in reverse – that is, from dark to light.
For example, apply opaque paint or 3D expanding medium as a patterning
device. 3D expanding medium can be pre-coloured or coloured when dry
with gilding waxes, interference paints and glitter to provide surface
dimension. Any other opaque medium, such as heavy-body acrylics, will
stand up against a dark background. Placing distressed pieces of Lutradur
over brightly coloured fabric will help to create more dimension and add a
backlighting effect, as Lutradur is translucent in nature.

BOW: Even charcoal-coloured Lutradur
still retains its transparency. After
being stamped with a fabric paint and
heat distressed, this sample was
placed over a gold mirror board.
20 x 20cm (7¾ x 7¾in)

RIGHT: As with the sample shown opposite, charcoal Lutradur comes alive with a bright orange lining.
20 x 20cm (7¾ x 7¾in)

Applying foils to Lutradur

If you have used a soldering iron to cut pieces of Lutradur, on close examination you will see that the edges are slightly raised because of the melting effect. If you then apply hot transfers foils to these edges (see page 29), they will adhere along the thickened edges. You can also apply sheets of foil to the surface of Lutradur, and the uppermost threads of the fabric will acquire traces of foil. The effect is very subtle, but works well with pieces that catch the light.

RIGHT: This detail demonstrates how the edges of Lutradur swell up when melted with a soldering iron. If a hot foil is laid over the top and pressed with an iron, the thickened edges with catch some of the foil.
5 x 5cm (2 x 2in)

RIGHT: Both Lutradur and Evolon were used here. The underlying Evolon was dyed and foiled with hot foils and an adhesive such as Bondaweb. Hot foils lose some of their lustre if subsequent heat is applied to the surface. The top layer is a piece of transfer-dyed 30gsm Lutradur, attached with both hand and machine stitches and overprinted with a foam stamp.

44 x 38cm (17 3/8 x 15in)

Size and scale

Size refers to overall dimensions; scale refers to the relative size of individual elements. The two kimono pieces shown here were created as a maquette and a full-sized piece of work, *Kimono Quilt*. It is obvious that the full-sized finished piece is not quite the same as the maquette. Both examples were an attempt to describe and highlight the potential pitfalls of working through ideas in small scale and then attempting to scale up for the final piece. I'm sure many students on creative textile courses have encountered this problem, and possibly ended up feeling inadequate, or at the very least dissatisfied, when the attempt fails. But take heart, it is almost impossible to work in small scale for fabric pieces, because it does not behave in miniature in the way that, for example, a sculptor can use clay or plaster to work out ideas for a larger sculpture in bronze. Scaling up ideas may involve exchanging a fine fabric for a heavier one, or including less detail but in larger scale.

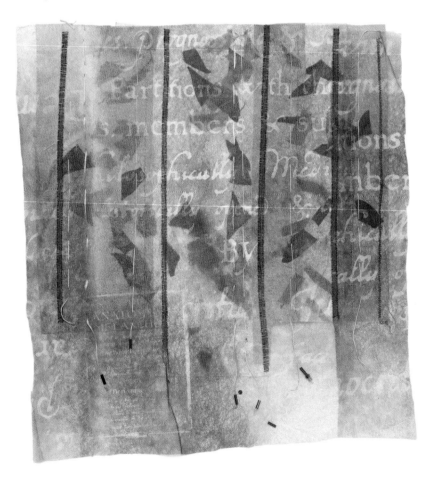

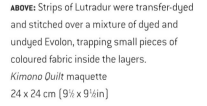

ABOVE: Strips of Lutradur were transfer-dyed and stitched over a mixture of dyed and undyed Evolon, trapping small pieces of coloured fabric inside the layers.
Kimono Quilt maquette
24 x 24 cm (9½ x 9½in)

RIGHT: The large kimono evolved from the maquette (shown left). Design elements such as text, stitching and details had to be adapted for the larger scale. Fabric also hangs differently when increased in size.
Kimono Quilt 110 x 90cm (43¼ x 35½in)

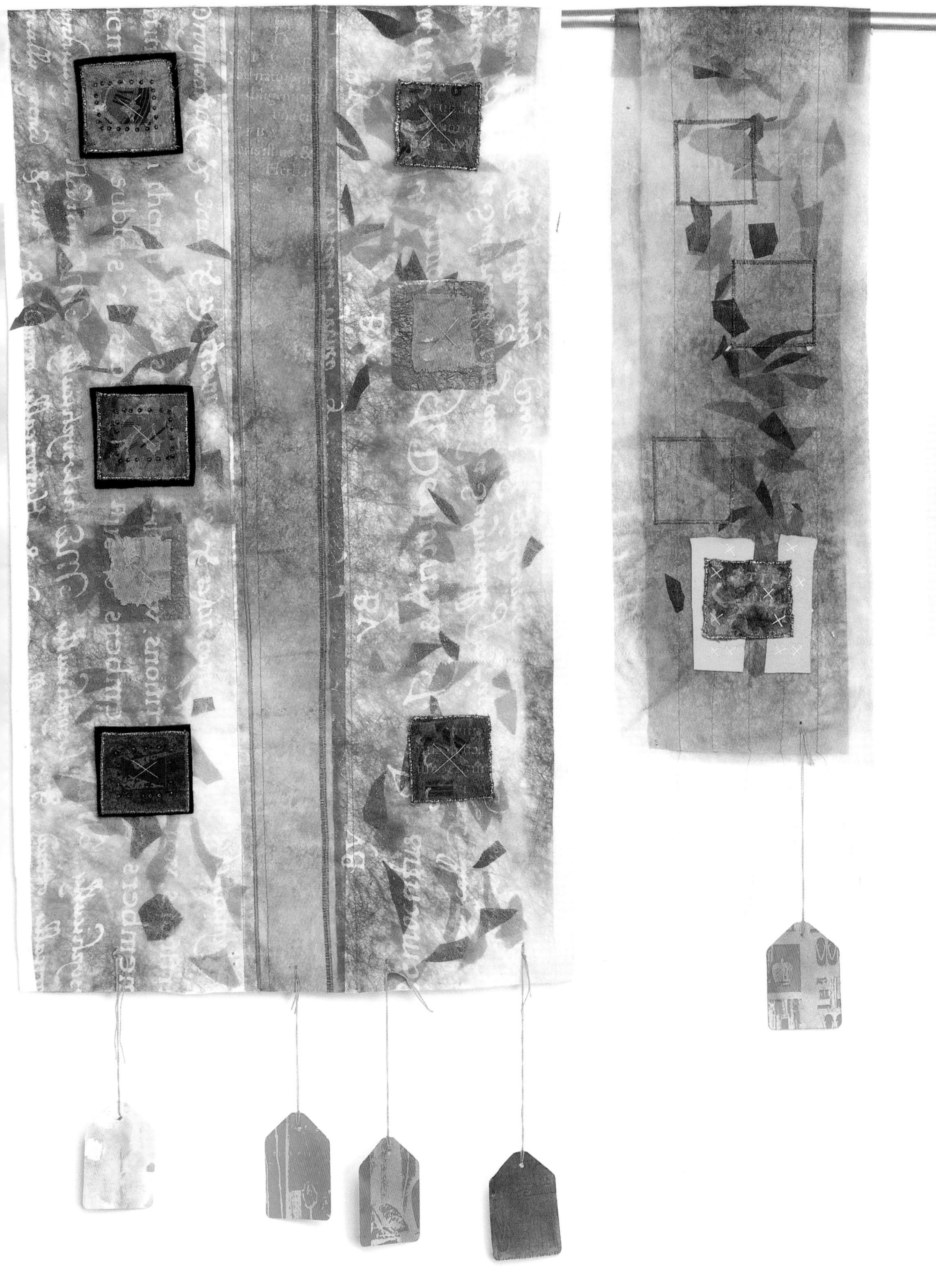

CRYSTAL SPUNBONDED POLYESTER

Similar to Lutradur in construction, crystal spunbonded polyester has a crisp finish, but can be scrunched up or softened by rubbing the fabric.

The 17gsm version gives a cobweb-like effect. It also has a tissue-like quality. Because of these two qualities it can easily be hand pleated and set in hot water, as demonstrated in the purple dress, shown opposite. It does, however, offer less resistance to being torn than Lutradur and has a hot calendered surface which creates the glossy crystal-like effect on the surface of the fabric.

The 70gsm is much more like Lutradur in structure, although it still has the crystal effect and a crisp handle. All of the techniques that can be applied to Lutradur can be applied to crystal spunbonded fabric.

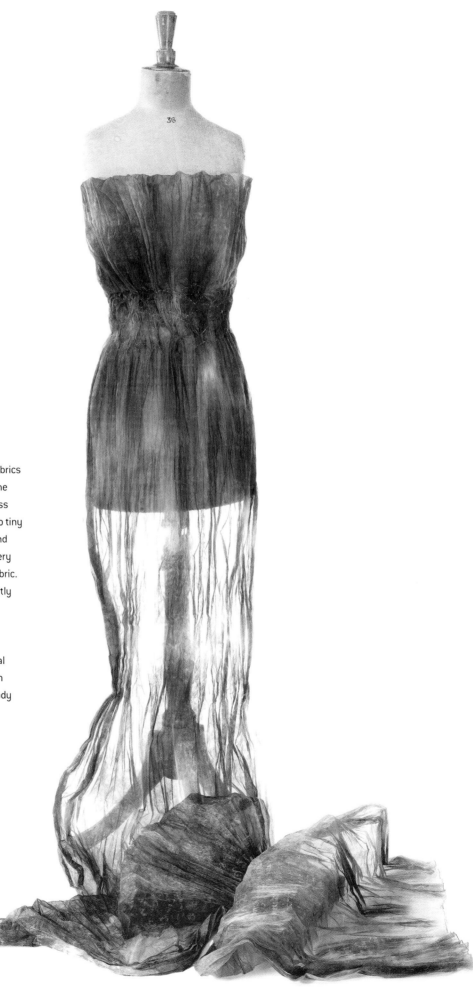

LEFT: Many of the lighter spunbonded fabrics lend themselves very easily to being fine pleated. The pleating on this purple dress was created by pulling the fabric up into tiny pleats by hand, wringing the fabric round into a hank, and then plunging it into very hot water; the creases 'cook' into the fabric. Once dry, all edges that are subsequently machine satin stitched will produce a clamshell-edge effect.

RIGHT: A long, continuous piece of crystal spunbonded polyester was printed with transfer dye and crumpled around a body form to suggest a 'dress'.

LEFT: Unlike many textile pieces, this work was mounted on canvas stretchers, starting with a plain-dyed piece of cotton muslin in quite a garish orange. All the subsequent pieces of fabric, which were printed through an inkjet printer, were laid on top. The uppermost layer is a piece of 17gsm crystal spunbonded fabric, which was coloured and printed using transfer-dye painted photocopies and then stretched onto the stretcher bars. Very tiny stitches were put in a grid formation to hold the fabric pieces in place.

There Are Places I Remember (detail)
(Mixed fabrics on stretcher bars, 2009)
60 x 60cm (24 x 24in)

ABOVE RIGHT: This piece is an amalgamation of many of the techniques described, such as transfer dyeing with a photocopy, using a soldering iron to create cut-out apertures, and using simple hand stitches as a means of assembly.
40 x 38cm (15¾ x 15in)

RIGHT: Very small pieces of lightweight crystal spunbonded fabric were machine satin stitched together with printed pieces of plain fabric and hand stitched into place on top of printed fabric.
18 x 18cm (7 x 7in)

EVOLON

Evolon is a spunlaced web consisting of continuous filaments. It is made from 70 per cent polyester and 30 per cent polyamide polymers, extruded as alternating segments in a single filament, which are split lengthwise using high-pressure water jets that tightly entangle and consolidate the filaments. This process enables the finished fabric to appear to have the qualities of paper or a paper-like structure, as with Evolon Original. Further washing processes produce the softer, brushed finish of Evolon Soft.

Evolon contains no binder or solvent, making it an eco-friendly alternative fabric. It provides ultraviolet protection and thermal insulation, can be ultrasonically cut, and is washable, breathable and quick drying. Having a superior mechanical construction, it will not loose its shape, but at the same time has soft drape and is lighter weight than its woven equivalents.

EVOLON ORIGINAL AND EVOLON SOFT

Evolon has two very different surfaces. Evolon Original is an unprocessed version, similar to a loomstate calico – in other words, how it comes off the production line. It has a stiffer feel and can be used in projects that need extra resiliance, such as three-dimensional objects.

Evolon Soft has been washed much like stonewashing silk to produce a very soft, drapable fabric with a surface similar to chamois leather. It is equally tough due to the spunbonded construction, which makes it a much more user-friendly fabric for everyday items such as bags, cushions, and even clothing as Evolon is also breathable. Excessive heat distressing will toughen up the fabric but it will remain workable.

As Evolon has proved to be popular, several other weights are planned, including 60, 130, and 170gsm in both original and soft finishes.

OPPOSITE AND BELOW: Several process were involved in creating the surface pattern on these book covers: transfer dyeing, inkjet printing and rubber stamping. The Evolon was left white, which makes any transfer dyes appear much brighter. The text was applied using the photocopy mask technique (see page 24). Two pieces of Evolon were printed through an inkjet printer to achieve additional patterning and finally overstamped with rubber stamps. 16 x 16cm (6¼ x 6¼in)

TECHNIQUES FOR WORKING WITH EVOLON

The same techniques can be applied to both Evolon and Evolon Soft.
They can be heat distressed, much like all of the other fabrics listed;
however, because of the nylon element, they will melt or cut at a higher
temperature than, say, Lutradur. In some ways this is all to the good,
as the burn or melt can be more easily controlled. Because Evolon is
a mixture of polyester and polyamide (nylon), it can be dip dyed in
hot-water acid dye.

Inkjet printing on Evolon

Both Evolon and Lutradur can be printed through an inkjet printer, as
detailed in the sections on colouring and printing techniques (see pages
20–25 and 31–35). However, because Evolon is highly absorbent it may
cause excessive printer ink to bleed before it has the chance to dry. My advice
is always first to try printing a fabric through a printer to see what happens
and then to address the issues that arise from your experiments. Treating
with Print.Ability will help prevent excessive ink bleeding into the Evolon.
Most fabrics require supporting to enable them to pass through a printer,
but otherwise, take this as your starting point.

LEFT: This is a composite piece, using
many techniques. The text section was
inkjet printed onto undyed Evolon Original,
then pieces of purple and bronze polyester
organza were stitched over the top and cut
with a soldering iron in a grid formation.
Pieces of the grid were gently teased
away from the surface to reveal parts
of the underlying text. The tags were made
from punched out pieces of card, painted
and stamped with 3D expanding medium,
and attached with machine stitching.
42 x 30cm (16½ x 11¾in)

RIGHT: Inkjet printing onto fabric is quite
straightforward and is described on pages
31–35. For this piece, dyed Evolon was
printed with a black-and-white image. A
piece of plain tissue paper was also printed
with a picture of some calligraphic text and
torn randomly along each edge. A piece
of torn polyester organza was stitched
through all layers and apertures cut out
with a soldering iron.
26 x 22cm (10¼ x 8⅝in)

Applying foils to Evolon

Applying transfer foils or hot foils to any fabric usually requires an adhesive such as Bondaweb to hold the foil. Hot foils can be applied to the surface of spunbonded fabric without the need for an adhesive. However, the surface is not very robust and can be removed by rubbing or through normal wear and tear if applied to a garment or bag. Evolon, in particular, accepts hot foils to its surface, but the transfer is an uncertain process and will give uneven results.

BELOW LEFT: This grey sample was created using an oil-on-water foil and the adhesive used was double-sided sticky tape. It was then distressed by subjecting the transferred foil to longer periods of heat from an iron. This technique has the effect of reducing some of the shine; the addition of iridescent mica powder enabled further shine to be removed to produce a subtle, distressed metallic effect and reduced the tackiness of the sticky tape.

BELOW RIGHT: Evolon was quilted to a piece of felt and hot foils applied to emphasize the quilt lines.
17 x 20cm (6⅝ x 7¾in)

BELOW: This bag is easier to make than it looks. Three rectangular pieces of dyed Evolon that are big enough to make a bag were layered and laid flat. Using a soldering iron and a metal rule, a grid was drawn across the surface of the topmost layer. The soldering iron was then pushed through the centre of each square, checking that all of the layers were fused together. The squares were separated by cutting through the top two layers with a pair of scissors. Hot foils were then randomly pressed across the surface.

Toner transfer printing on Evolon

Copier toner can be transferred to Evolon either by using heat (as described on page 38) or by using a solvent (as described on page 56), in the same way as it can be transferred to Lutradur. As explained earlier in the book, each method will produce slightly unpredicatable results and the one you opt for is a matter of personal choice. On the example shown here, acetone was used to transfer laser-printed architectural details randomly across the surface of dyed Evolon.

Copier toner also has an affinity for transfer foil. Different methods of applying transfer (hot) foils have been described for several pieces in this book, but here a novel application has been used to heat transfer the foil to toner which has itself first been transferred onto the fabric surface – look closely at the door and brickwork images.

LEFT AND RIGHT: This piece was created in the same way as the piece featuring St Paul's Cathedral (see page 39), using a combination of laser photocopy transfers, soldering, transfer dyes and appliquéing polyester organza with a soldering iron. Where a laser photocopy has been transferred to synthetic fabric, hot foils will adhere to the toner that has transferred – not perfectly, but producing an interesting random effect.

22 x 20cm (8⅝ x 7¾in)

Welding and soldering Evolon

Evolon can be cut with a soldering iron but, because of the tougher polyamide fibres, it offers a little more resistance than other spunbonded materials such as Lutradur. This can be used to good effect. When a fabric such as polyester organza is placed over the top and cut with a soldering iron, the organza will cut easily and will become welded to the Evolon as the shapes are cut out.

BELOW: For this bag, layers of Evolon and Kunin felt were laid on top of each other and machine stitched in a grid formation. A hot soldering iron was used to cut through both layers of fabric in a repeat pattern. Beads were stitched on for detail across the surface of the fabric and a beaded tassel added for decoration.

RIGHT: Evolon was printed through an inkjet printer to form the background image, then a separate piece of Evolon was printed with images of butterflies and cut out with a soldering iron. The butterfly-printed fabric was then stitched onto the background fabric with machine stitching.

5 x 5cm (2 x 2in)

BELOW: The fabrics used in this piece are Evolon Soft and polyester organza. The petals were created by sandwiching the two fabrics together in an embroidery hoop. Using a paper template and a soldering iron, the two fabrics were cut out and welded together at the same time. The petals, increasing in size, were stitched onto a padded square of Evolon, starting from the centre and moving outwards.

Stamping on Evolon

Although a fabric with a discernable 'surface', Evolon is capable of accommodating rubber stamping very well as it captures even very fine detail. Foam stamps are also a very useful tool for creating less-defined shapes for backgrounds and general repeat patterns.

RIGHT: This sample has been pre-dyed, stamped with a foam stamp and various paints and then stamped using bleach to discharge some of the colour from the dyed Evolon.
50 x 50cm (19¾ x 19¾in)

BELOW: Acid-dyed Evolon Original was used as the basis for this bag. Water-based paint and a foam stamp created the surface decoration, followed by a machine satin stitch. The whole piece was then placed in an embroidery hoop and heat distressed with a heat gun. Finally, small sections of fused Angelina fibre and crystal organza were used to create the bag lining.
15 x 13cm (6 x 5in)

LEFT: The soldering iron can be used as a tool to create decorative effects even just by using the simplest of the tips. This sample has been used to create a perforated edge around the butterfly which is an image used from a CD-ROM of images and backgrounds. 9 x 6cm (3½ x 2⅜in)

Pleating Evolon

Creating surfaces does not necessarily consist of adding other elements: the base fabric itself can be used. Being a thermoplastic fabric, Evolon can be pleated or scrunched simply by immersing it in very hot water. Have you ever 'overcooked' a polyester garment in a tumble drier for it to be forever creased? This is the same effect, but applied with a degree of control.

BELOW: The Evolon was pre-dyed, pleated up in the fingertips and then rolled into a twist. It was left in boiling water for long enough for the water to penetrate, then removed from the water and dried while still pleated. This sample then had gold foil randomly applied across the surface. 20 x 12cm (8 x 4¾in)

Heat embossing Evolon

Because Evolon has a higher melting temperature than most other spunbonded fabrics additional techniques, such as heat embossing with embossing powders, can be used to embellish the surface.

To apply heat embossing to Evolon, place it into an embroidery hoop to keep the fabric flat while you are working. You can then apply any ink pads, embossing ink pads or even paints to the surface of the Evolon. Sprinkle on embossing powders and heat distress in the same way that you would when working on paper – the embossing powder will melt to form a slightly raised surface.

HEAT-DISTRESSABLE TISSUE

The newest heat-distressable fabric on the market is heat-distressable tissue (17gsm), which is made from polyester although not from a continuous filament. Heat-distressable tissue is quite similar to paper, but almost unique in that it will heat distress and remain paper-like throughout.

TECHNIQUES FOR WORKING WITH HEAT-DISTRESSABLE TISSUE

Heat-distressable tissue responds to heat in a very similar way to Tyvek (see pages 100–101), by producing a 'bubbled' surface. Unlike Tyvek, however, it remains tissue-like after being dyed and distressed and can therefore be stitched either before or after heating. It is far less likely to tear when machine stitched, although will tear easily along one grain. Tearing across the other grain will produce a postage-stamp style edge.

Colouring heat-distressable tissue

Heat-distressable tissue can be coloured in exactly the same way as Lutradur but, as it is hydrophobic, it cannot absorb moisture (such as water-based paints or ink). If Print.Ability (see page 12) is painted or sprayed onto the surface, the ink will become fixed. Other printing aids can be used, but will leave a stiff residue and cannot be subsequently heat distressed.

RIGHT: This piece has been heat distressed with a heat gun and sprayed with dye-based sprays containing mica powder, which emphasizes the undulations of the fabric.
21 x 21cm (8¼ x 8¼in)

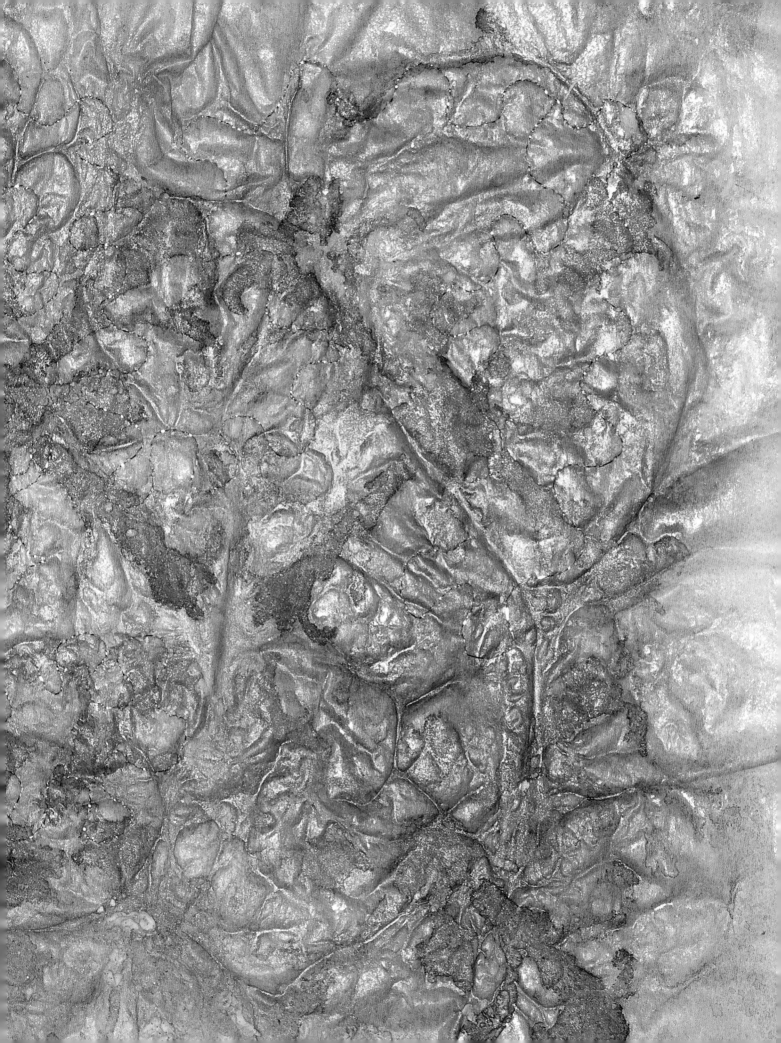

Stamping heat-distressable tissue

Any of the print techniques described in this book, including stamping, can
be used on heat-distressable tissue. Heat-distressable tissue can also be printed
through an inkjet printer. As with regular tissue paper, you will need to support it
on freezer paper to enable it to travel through the printer. Heat-distressable tissue
has a smooth and a dull side, either of which can be printed on, but it needs to be
pre-treated with a printing aid such as Print.Ability to stabilize dye-based inks.

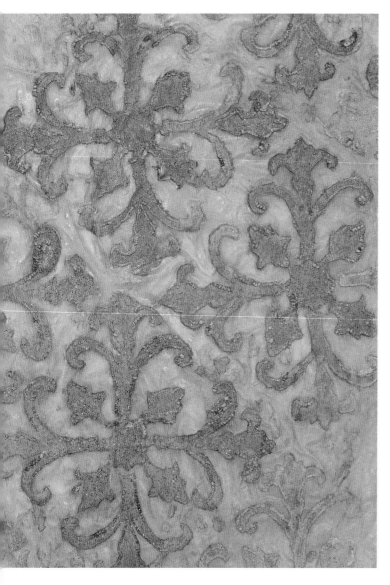

ABOVE: 3D expanding medium was stamped
onto the surface of the tissue and then
coloured with random colours of dye-based
spritzes and walnut ink, together with very
small amounts of glitter and mica powder.
20 x 28cm (8 x 11in)

ABOVE: This piece was printed with 3D
expanding medium and spritzed with
dye-based sprays. The tissue was held in an
embroidery hoop during heat distressing to
keep the resulting fabric flat (note where
the tissue has split as a result).
20 x 28cm (8 x 11in)

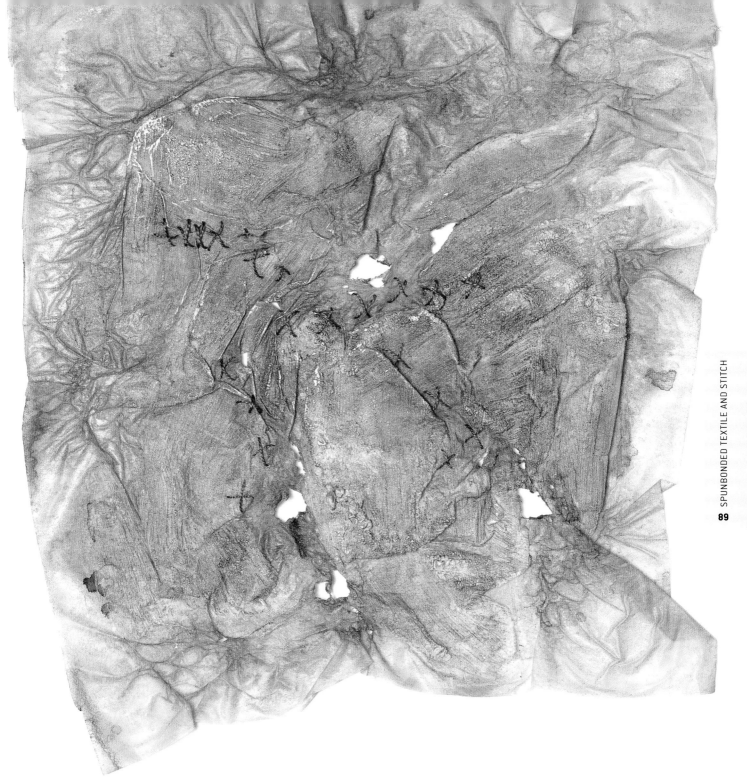

ABOVE: Very dimensional surfaces can be created by using varying amounts of 3D expanding medium. This example has been painted with thick amounts of 3D expanding medium, so that the brush marks are still visible, and heat distressed randomly across the surface. After heating, the surface was treated with walnut ink and mica powders.

20 x 20cm (8 x 8in)

Distressing heat-distressable tissue

Treating the surface of heat-distressable tissue with heat using a heat tool produces a mottled effect like a faux crocodile skin although, unlike Tyvek, the fabric remains very fine and tissue-like. Dye-based sprays or liquid paint will run into the valleys created by heat distressing, helping to define the patterning as in the sample above.

Solder distressing heat-distressable tissue

A soldering iron is mostly used as a cutting tool but here is has been used as a texturing tool by gently brushing it across the surface of the tissue. If small pieces of the tissue are placed on other spunbonded fabrics they will fuse together.

RIGHT: Here, small strips of sprayed tissue have been placed onto Lutradur and a soldering iron used to cut across the tissue and fuse both fabrics. The holes were created by pushing a soldering iron through all layers of fabric. A red backing fabric provides depth and colour.

ABOVE: This sample was stamped, coloured and heat distressed. It was then stitched onto Kunin felt to lift the colour and expose small areas of colour when distressed with a soldering iron.

RIGHT: This sample was stamped, coloured and heat distressed before being placed onto Lutradur XL. The soldering iron marks achieve very fine tip marks — a good technique to give surface variation and add dimension.

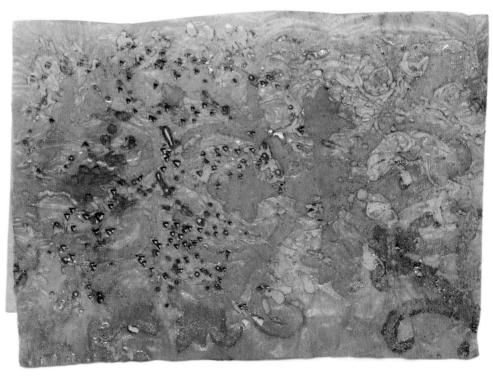

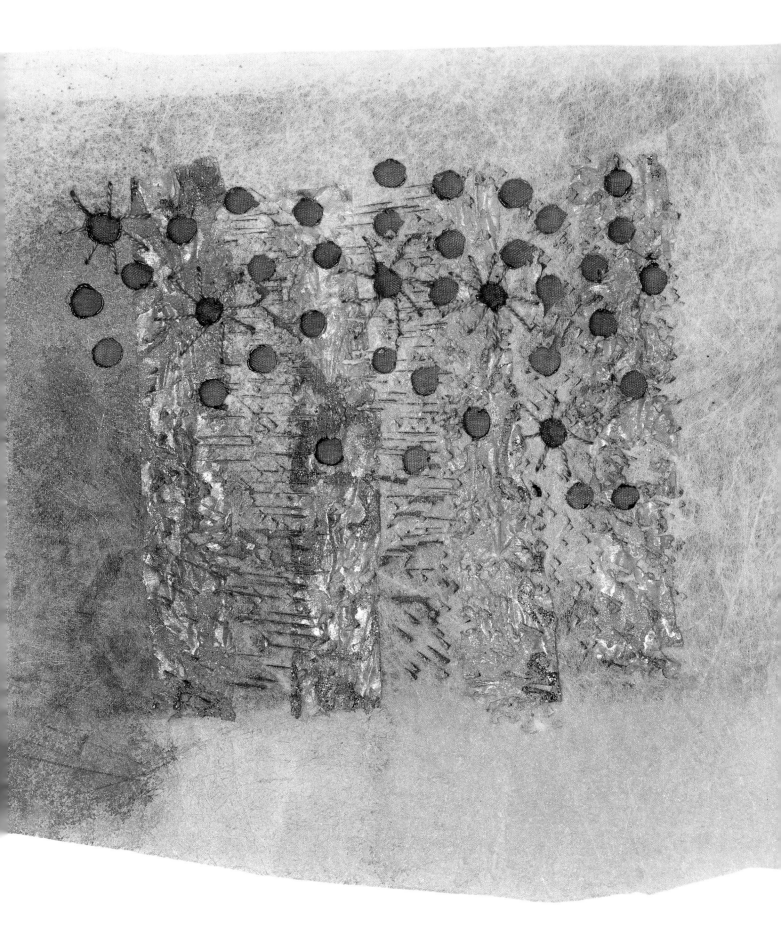

Stitching heat-distressable tissue

Because heat-distressable tissue is very fine it can be machine stitched very easily, even when placed on a layer of Lutradur XL or other firm fabric.

Although ordinary paper can be stitched by hand or by machine, there are pitfalls to avoid. A line of stitching in paper will create a 'tear-off' line that substantially weakens the surface. Heat-distressable tissue will not tear around stitching because of the inherent toughness of the polyester fibres and, despite having many similarities to paper, it will drape and bend to form soft, sculpted pieces.

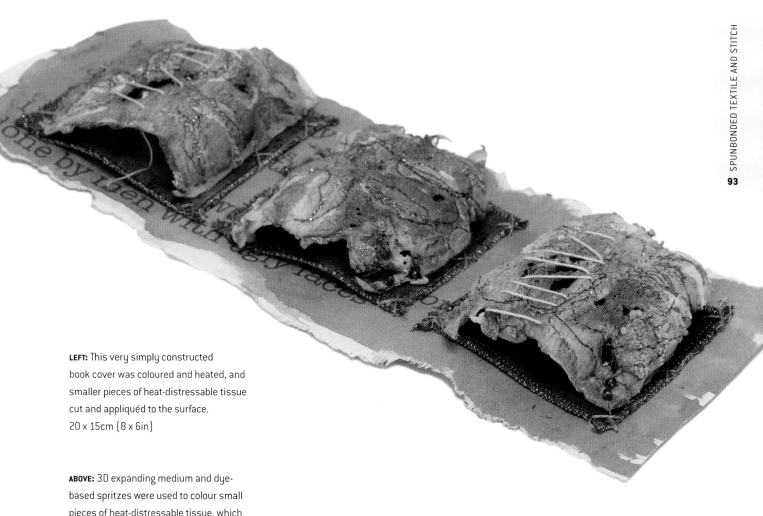

LEFT: This very simply constructed book cover was coloured and heated, and smaller pieces of heat-distressable tissue cut and appliquéd to the surface.
20 x 15cm (8 x 6in)

ABOVE: 3D expanding medium and dye-based spritzes were used to colour small pieces of heat-distressable tissue, which were then machine stitched to Lutradur XL. Heat distressing the piece has caused the Lutradur to curl. The three small pieces were placed on top of coloured fabric squares on a paper background for contrast.
12 x 30cm (4¾ x 12in)

Blue dress

This dress was constructed from a simple pattern, the skirt being cut from just two rectangular pieces of heat-distressable tissue. All the dress pieces were stamped in an all-over pattern using a foam stamp and a very thin pressing of 3D expanding medium. When the medium had dried, the tissue was sprayed with a thin film of Print.Ability, to help retain the layer of dye-based spray that was then sprayed over all the pieces. The tissue was then heat distressed with a heat gun, causing the surface to waffle very gently. The tulle underskirts are made from nylon dyed with hot-water acid dye.

The bag was created in the same way as the dress. It is formed of one rectangular piece of heat-distressable tissue, which was pre-decorated with 3D expanding medium and dye-based spray-on colours as described above.

BELOW: The tissue for this purse was prepared in exactly the same as the fabric for the dress (opposite), but extra-fine colours and details were applied over the surface.

RIGHT: Making a dress from paper is not a new idea, but this one demonstrates the best of both worlds – a material that is as strong as fabric but as wispy as paper.

TYVEK

Tyvek was first developed in 1955 as a result of a chance discovery when white polyethylene fibres were found coming out of a pipe in a DuPont laboratory, leading to Tyvek becoming a registered trademark of DuPont in 1967, when the first trial fabrics were produced.

Tyvek is made of pure high-density polyethylene (HDPE) fibres, which are very fine 0.5–0.10mm fibres (human hair is about 0.75mm in cross section). These fibres are first spun and then bonded together by heat and pressure, without binders. It is 100 per cent recyclable just like plastic bottles and, as an added bonus, is itself being produced using 25 per cent PCR (post-consumer recycled) material.

Tyvek is available in both 'paper' and 'fabric' versions. Both types have high opacity, excellent whiteness, good printability and can resist repeated folding and flexing without tearing.

The hard-structure 'paper' version has a rough, or 'wire', side and a smooth side. The difference is minor, but can usually be felt, and can be seen easily under a low-power magnifying glass. The smooth side should be used for print clarity. 'Paper' Tyvek is coated on one side with an antistatic agent to aid handling, but this can be removed with distilled water.

The soft-structure 'fabric' type has a linen structure on one side and rib on the reverse. The linen side is preferred for printing because it holds the ink better and has better surface fibre stability. The linen side is also smoother than the rib side.

TECHNIQUES FOR WORKING WITH TYVEK

If there is one criticism to be made of Tyvek, it is that it becomes very hard after being heat distressed. Because of this quality, many of the pieces that are made from Tyvek can look very similar. Tyvek also shrinks very easily when subjected to heat, and many of the following samples have explored this quality.

Both fabric and paper Tyvek have very different but equally pleasing if unusual surfaces and handling, so explore this to its best advantage.

ABOVE: Tyvek fabric was coloured using an inkjet printer and Print.Ability was used to fix the ink. It was then quilted onto a piece of felt and combined with strips of frayed and rolled polyester organza and bamboo skewers. The pins hold the piece in place on the backing.
29 x 21cm (11½ x 8¼in)

Using Tyvek with other fabrics

Some of the heat-distressed samples featured on the following pages may look quite dull to the uninitiated, but for those who are interested in creating surface texture, Tyvek is an unsung hero that is often used to create raised surfaces on regular fabrics (see page 101).

Adhesives

A number of adhesives can be used to glue Tyvek, either to itself or to other fabrics. Fast-drying water-based adhesives are preferable, as synthetic adhesives can act as solvents at higher temperatures, causing swelling and wrinkling. Hot-melt EVA (amber-coloured glue stick) adhesives or sticky tape can also be used effectively.

Sewing Tyvek

Tyvek can be machine stitched, with the best results being obtained from machines equipped with drop-feeds, as the metal feed dogs tend to leave impressions on the surface. When stitching Tyvek, use the least number of stitches per inch (your largest stitches) and the smallest needle practical for maximum resistance to tearing.

Inkjet printing and dyeing Tyvek

Tyvek can be inkjet printed using pigmented water-based inks, but conventional textile-dyeing processes do not impart permanent colour to Tyvek. Sublimation dyes (transfer dyes) can be used, but caution is required because of the higher temperatures needed.

Dye-based sprays or inkjet ink can be applied in the same way as to other spunbonded fabrics, but require an ink stabilizer, such as Print.Ability, to hold the ink as it dries.

RIGHT: This piece was created using Evolon and an inkjet printer. The Print.Ability helps to stabilize the printed image to enable it to dry and the same technique can be used with Tyvek. The faux quilting was created using a soldering iron.
29 x 21cm (11½ x 8¼in)

Heat distressing Tyvek

For most textile artists, the favourite method of treating Tyvek is to distress the surface with heat, using either a heat gun or a household iron.

Heat from a gun will distress the surface and shrink it very quickly, so a little practice is needed to perfect the burning. If holes are required, then placing Tyvek fabric in an embroidery hoop will make the fabric split into holes rather than shrink.

An alternative, particularly for Tyvek paper, is to use an iron. Placing a piece of Tyvek on or near the plate of an iron will make the surface bubble. Any surface embellishment or colouring is best applied before heating as the Tyvek paper becomes very hard. Any bubbling in the surface of Tyvek will always form away from the direction of the heat.

BELOW LEFT: Here Tyvek fabric has been distressed with a heat gun and left unsupported. The air from the gun was wafted up and down the fabric in straight lines to produce a seersucker effect. 25 x 20cm (10 x 8in)

BELOW RIGHT: Tyvek fabric placed in an embroidery hoop and heat distressed with a gun can only shrink and pull away from the heat, creating holes in the fabric. 25 x 24cm (10 x 9½in)

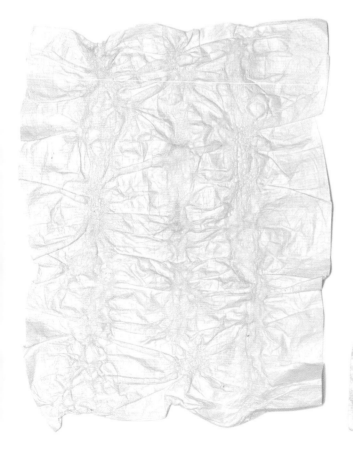

RIGHT: In these samples, the use of Tyvek is not at all obvious as it was used as a backing for polyester taffeta. The Tyvek was stitched to the back of the taffeta, either in rows or as a grid, and the heat from a heat gun shrank the Tyvek to produce a 'cloque' effect – a raised effect that looks similar to animal skin.
20 x 20cm (8 x 8in)

Using printing aids with Tyvek

One of the main industrial applications for Tyvek is printing for banners. The commercial process uses industrial inks, but it can be adapted for small-scale craft use. By using a printing aid, the surface can accept inkjet inks onto its otherwise smooth surface. The following pieces were made from Tyvek fabric and pre-coloured using an inkjet printer.

RIGHT: I found a small watercolour in an old sketchbook and scanned it into my computer. Printing the image onto fabric Tyvek produced a faithful representation of the original painting.
20 x 21cm (8 x 8¼in)

BELOW: Tyvek fabric is soft enough to create a faux nappa leather if stitched to another soft fabric such as felt. Again, the colour was created by printing using an inkjet printer and was softly enhanced with gilding ink.
10 x 24cm (4 x 9½in)

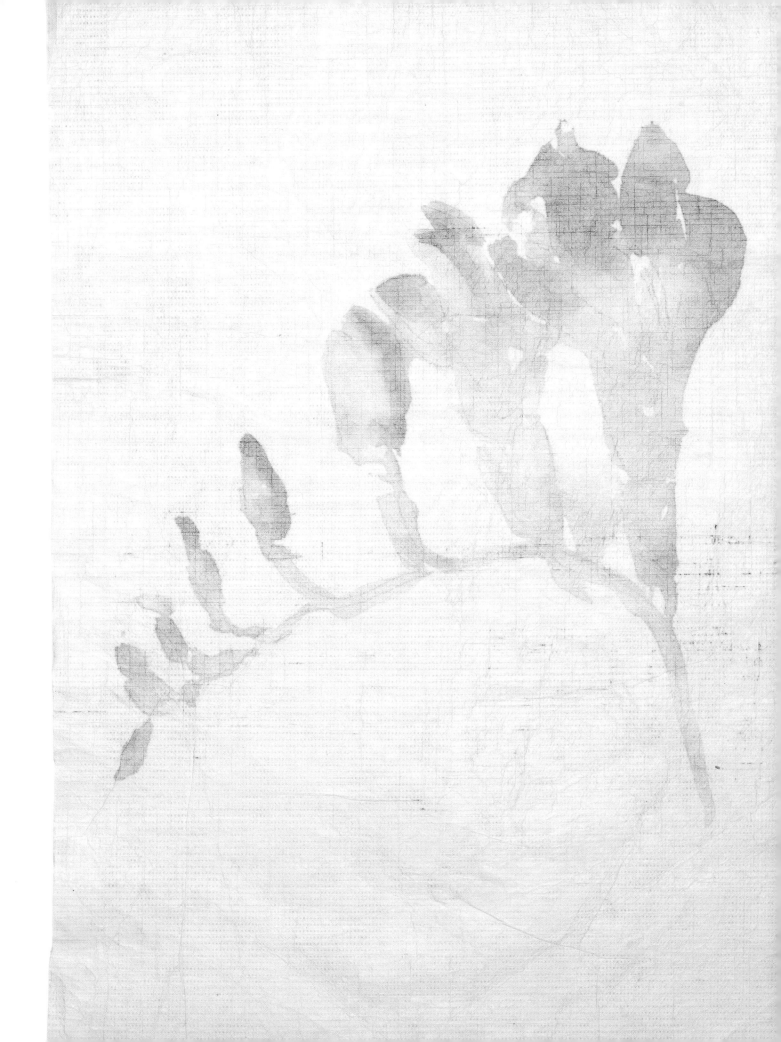

KUNIN FELT

Kunin felt is a trademark that has been adopted as the generic term for this kind of felt and is made from 100 per cent polyester (not acrylic or other mixes, as widely quoted). Polyester responds more readily to heat distressing, as evidenced by other fabrics in this book. Acrylic will melt, albeit at higher temperatures, but it will form a solid residue; polyester dissipates more readily to leave very little residue.

Kunin and other polyester felts are available in many colours, but some colours – for example, Kunin Scarlet Red – do not respond to heat distressing. Marled colours plus black and white are generally very reliable.

TECHNIQUES FOR WORKING WITH KUNIN FELT

At first glance, felt is an unsophisticated product and not a likely bedfellow for fine-art textiles. Moreover, the duller the colour, the less 'shelf appeal' it has. However, it is a perfect foil for dimensional distressed effects, particularly for medieval, gothic or rustic themes.

Simple heat distressing

The mottled colours give the most interesting results as the colour is not flat, which helps to create depth. Heat distress the surface just gently and you will get a simple, fairly even pattern. Once the surface has cooled, it will feel quite rough; this surface lends itself to being lightly rubbed with coloured products such as gilding wax, which will highlight not only the surface texture but also the patterning.

For a more structured pattern, a stencil system of some kind should be used as a patterning device. You can create your own stencil by cutting into paper, acetate or Mylar with a craft knife or a soldering iron; otherwise, cut or tear a pattern into some freezer paper. To ensure that your distressed felt does not fall apart entirely, make sure that your pattern markings are touching.

LEFT: A simple snowflake stencil was used to create random motifs across the surface using PVA glue. Glitter has been added and then gently heat distressed.

Patterning Kunin felt

Place a stencil on the felt, securing it at each corner. You then need to select a product such as fabric paint, acrylic paint, 3D expanding medium, or any wet medium, as this is the mechanism by which the resistance to the heat is created. Place a small puddle of paint at the edge of the stencil. Using a spatula, pull the paint from this reservoir across the surface of the felt at an angle of approximately 45 degrees (any steeper or shallower will cause the paint to bleed under the edges of the stencil or not cover evenly enough – a technique similar to that of screen printing). Heat distress over the paint.

If you use 3D expanding medium, this will give you an opaque finish (usually white) and will allow you to add contrasting colour to the surface pattern. PVA glue will create very translucent pattern markings and pearlized paints give an effect somewhere between the two. In addition to the paint or medium, you could add embossing powder at the same time in order to obtain a more raised or metallic finish.

Dimensional fabric paints are a very good medium to use, particularly as most of these products come in a tube with a needle-tip applicator. This will enable you to trail a pattern on the felt in a controlled way. The paint needs to be applied quite thickly for a good result. Most paints will bubble – but some will give a glossy polished finish. If the dimensional paint is allowed to dry for a few hours, the felt will absorb much of the paint and much of the raised pearlized or metallic effect will be absorbed. All is not lost, however; if this does happen, the pattern resist will still be present.

RIGHT: Viscose thread has been used to stitch this piece of felt. Cotton and silk are a good alternative. However, do not use a polyester thread until you have tried a few test pieces, as this fibre will melt along with the felt. The stitching lines create the mask and heat from a heat gun will melt away the felt leaving only stitching.
25 x 15cm (10 x 6in)

BELOW LEFT: Kunin felt patterned with sparkly fabric paint applied through a stencil and heat distressed.
20 x 20cm (8 x 8in)

BELOW RIGHT: Kunin felt painted with fabric paint and heat distressed. Gilding wax was then rubbed lightly across the surface.
20 x 20cm (8 x 8in)

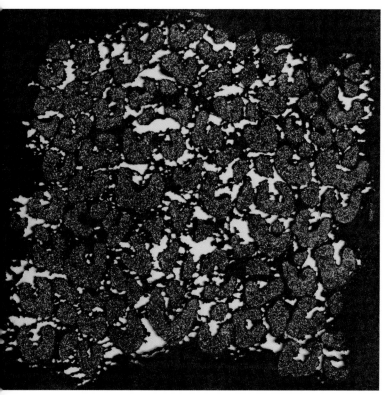

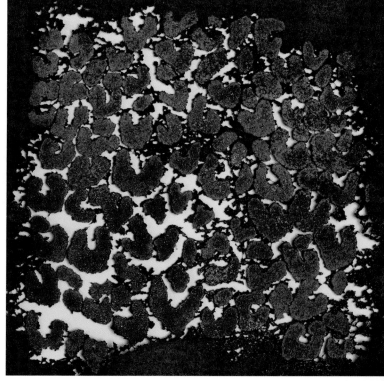

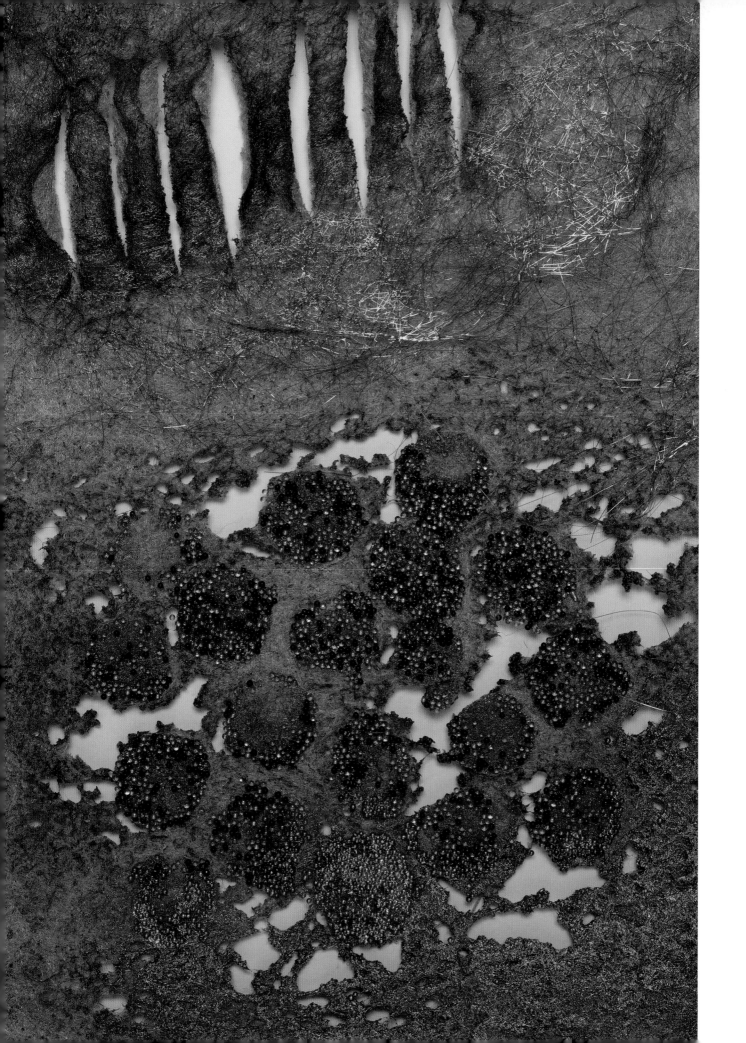

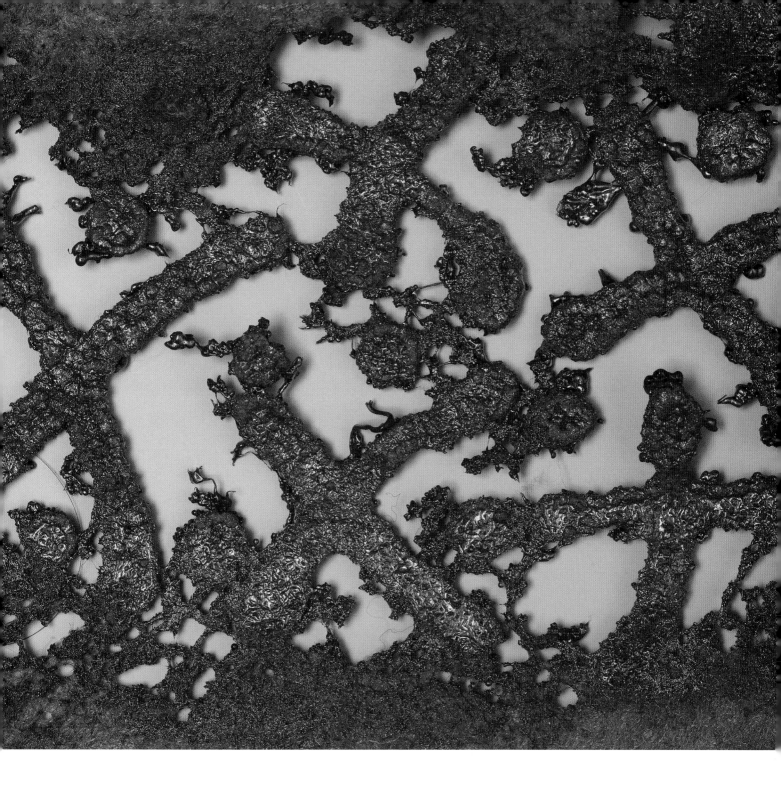

LEFT: At the top, strands of Angelica fibre have been laid across the Kunin felt, slashed with scissors through both layers and heat distressed. At the bottom, small dabs of PVA glue have been brushed onto the felt surface and small holeless beads sprinkled onto the wet glue. Heat distressing was applied while the glue was still wet.
8 x 5cm (3 x 2in)

ABOVE: Cross motifs were 'drawn' onto the surface of the felt using PVA glue. After heat distressing, gold-leaf paint was applied to the crosses.
10 x 15cm (4 x 6in)

Making three-dimensional objects

If you are making a three-dimensional piece and want some body in the felt, try applying acrylic ink to the moulded felt, either painting it onto the surface or applying it with a dropper. The ink will absorb readily, and when it has dried, the felt will have acquired a more cardboard-like form. Please note that this is not reversible! Applying a wash of acrylic paint or PVA glue will have the same effect.

BELOW: The image on this bag was created by pulling a very thin layer of 3D expanding medium through a stencil. When dry, the medium was enhanced with layers of acrylic metallic paints and dabs of glitter for highlights. 17 x 17cm (6¾ x 6¾in)

BELOW: These three samples demonstrate how Kunin felt distresses with heat and how to isolate a shape formed from a stamp motif with acrylic paint.

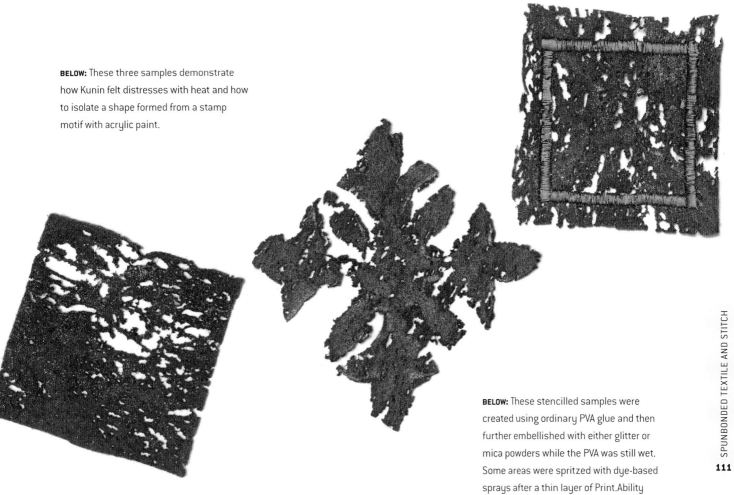

BELOW: These stencilled samples were created using ordinary PVA glue and then further embellished with either glitter or mica powders while the PVA was still wet. Some areas were spritzed with dye-based sprays after a thin layer of Print.Ability was applied.

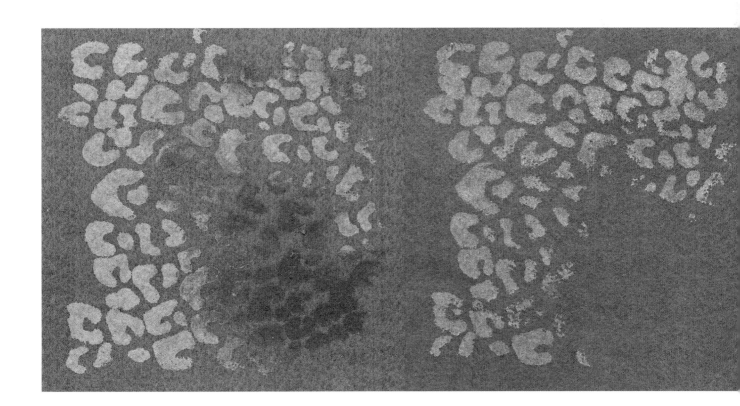

NAPPY LINER

Nappy liner was one of the first spunbonded fabrics to be used in creative textiles. The spun fibres are needle punched from polypropylene fibre and, as the fabric is very sensitive to heat distressing, great care must be taken to hold a heat gun well away from the surface and to waft it very freely across the surface as polypropylene starts to shrink and pull away at around 70°C (158°F). Distressed nappy liner mostly needs to be mounted on another fabric, as it becomes very fragile.

This fabric is available in 17, 30, 40, 50 and 100gsm although only the 17 and 30gsm versions are recognisable as nappy liner, as the heavier weights are much stiffer and denser. The lighter weights have a softer handle than any of the other spunbonded fabrics.

Nappy liner can be used to great effect to create small embellishments including handmade beads by wrapping long strips of coloured nappy liner around a small matchstick and heat distressing. The distressing glues the fabric bead together.

RIGHT: Nappy liner has been randomly stamped with 3D expanding medium and, when dry, sprayed with a solution of Print.Ability, which helps a walnut ink spray to adhere to the surface. The Print.Ability also allows the walnut ink to show up strongly, as it would otherwise be very pale.

BELOW: This simple piece of work was created in the same way as the piece shown opposite, but mounted onto tulle and then onto a piece of foam and moulded into a tube to form a small vessel.

Green dress

Although this dress is made from dyed Evolon Soft, it has a central panel of nappy liner that has been stamped with a very thin layer of 3D expanding medium and gently heat distressed. Both Evolon and nappy liner cling together very easily and the front panel of the dress has been embellished with simple hand stitches and applied crystal stones. While the 3D expanding medium was still wet, a tiny amount of glitter was sprinkled over the surface and remained fixed in place once the medium was dry. Heat distressing was then carried out. Additional embellishing consisting of random cross stitches and ribbons helps to add further dimension.

RIGHT: Evolon can be cut without any fraying or shedding of fibres so this dress has no hems, neck or armhole facings. Nappy liner works very well with Evolon and here provides the stunning embellishment on the central panel.

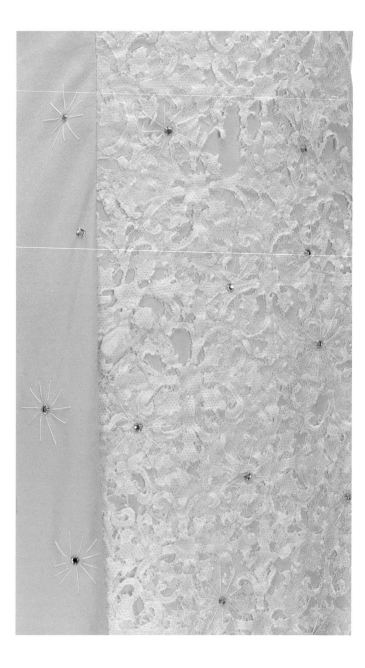

LEFT: A close-up detail of the centre panel demonstrates the dimensional effect achieved by the distressed nappy liner and how small, random hand stitching helps to secure the applied fabric.

SPUNBONDED TEXTILE AND STITCH

115

EXPERIMENTING FURTHER

The textile pieces in this book demonstrate elements that have always been evident in all of my work. To attempt to put these themes into some kind of context, I have included paintings, prints, and photographs, some of which were created over twenty years ago; when looking at them alongside my recent textile pieces, however, they could have been made yesterday, and I continue to explore the same themes and issues.

PHOTOGRAPHIC IMAGES

A desktop printer was used to create photographic images on fabric for many of the pieces in this book, but the digital age has seen the demise of both capturing photographs onto film and printing onto photographic paper in a darkroom. Paradoxically, then, you may be surprised to learn that I am a big advocate of creating images on film. The continuous-tone image still has a place and the darkroom will never fail to deliver that sense of surprise and delight. Anyone who has ever developed and printed a photograph in a darkroom knows that feeling of anticipation as the image slowly reveals itself through the ripples of a bath of developer. Moreover, the images here did not even require a camera to record them.

Photograms

Photograms are created by placing an object directly onto a piece of photographic paper and exposing the whole thing to light and, with the appropriate darkroom facilities, can be carried out either as a black-and-white or colour process.

ABOVE LEFT: Using a solid object for a photogram produces a solid outline, whereas translucent objects create images that contain variety in tone and shading.
Freesia (Cibachrome, 1992)
7 x 7cm (2¾ x 2¾in)

LEFT: Photograms of photographed images create an object acting as a negative. Solid objects create solid outlines.
Anemone 2
15 x 10cm (6 x 4in)

ABOVE: Like the colour photogram below, translucent objects such as petals allow varying amounts of light to be exposed onto photographic paper.
Alstromeria (Ilford Multigrade, 1992)
12 x 17cm (4¾ x 6⅝in)

LEFT: The background in this image was created using folded organza.
Anemone 6 (Cibachrome 1992)
17 x 12cm (6⅝ x 4¾in)

Gum bichromate printing

This image was created using one of the oldest photographic processes from the 19th century. Gum bichromate printing requires a large film negative, but otherwise the image is created using watercolour paints, a few light-sensitive chemicals (potassium dichromate), gum arabic and sunlight. This process can easily be reproduced on fabric. For more information on this specialist technique, see Further Reading (page 126).

Light-sensitive emulsion

Another photographic material that strays from the norm is light-sensitive emulsion, which is painted onto paper (or canvas on stretcher bars in this case) and processed in the normal way under darkroom conditions. Again, this process can be carried out on fabric – although, like acrylic mediums, it does leave a residue on fabric. For more information see Further Reading (page 126).

ABOVE: Old photographic processes usually produce images about the size of a negative. The negative for this image was created on a 20 x 28cm (8 x 11in) piece of film.
Rose 1 (Gum dichromate print on Arches Rives 300gsm watercolour paper, 1997)
20x 28cm (8 x 11in)

RIGHT: Traditional photographic paper is pre-coated with a silver-based emulsion, but liquid emulsions can be painted onto a surface of your choice, as here with broad brushstrokes onto paper.
Rose 2 (Light-sensitive emulsion on Fabriano watercolour paper, 1993)
35 x 25cm (13¾ x 10in)

THEMES

We all develop consistent themes that reappear time and time again, possibly without us even realizing it. It may be that we are interested in and enjoy experimenting with a particular technique, motif or colour, or our subconscious keeps returning to the same place in our memory. If you identify these themes it may help you to develop new work, but don't think about it too hard as it can also inhibit style and creativity.

LEFT: A detail of a sketch using wax crayons and ink overprinted with a black-and-white image using an inkjet printer.
Through the Looking Glass (inkjet printing over oil pastel on paper, 2008)
25 x 18cm (10 x 7in)

ABOVE: A similar layering effect to the piece shown opposite can be achieved by using photocopies or printable acetate, although photographic film creates denser areas of black and preserves grey scale.
How Does Your Garden Grow? (photographic film over oil on paper, 1991)
35 x 50cm (13¾ x 20in)

Layers

Transparent layers are a recurrent theme in many of my textile pieces and the transparencies used in the piece shown above are images created on black-and-white photographic film. Unlike photocopies, the grey scale maintains close-up detail. Layers are an over-riding theme in all of my work.

Layering for impact

In so many of the fabric pieces in this book, impact is created or enhanced by placing one translucent layer over another or against a strong colour. But unlike these photographic pieces, fabric layering makes the viewer work harder to discover the hidden image.

Frames and apertures

Many people assume that a work of art needs a frame in order to validate it, and there is no doubt that a frame can certainly add cohesion. Another recurring theme in my work is the presence of frames – or, as I prefer to regard them, apertures. One definition of an aperture is 'an opening that limits the amount of light that can pass through'. For me, an aperture within a composition adds a point of reference for the other elements. It acknowledges both the viewer and to the world outside the picture.

BELOW LEFT: *So Many People in the World Want to Cry* (oil on paper, 1991) 50 x 30cm (20 x 12in)

BELOW RIGHT: *I Have Seen Flowers Come In Stony Places* (photographic film over oil on paper, 1991) 60 x 40cm (24 x 16in)

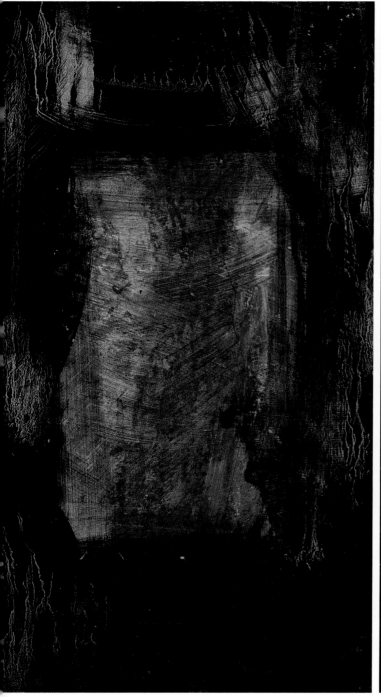

Crosses

X marks the spot…
is a sign of illiteracy
for no publicity
where two lines cross
a crossroads
erasure by typewriter
roman ten
24th letter of the alphabet
a windmill ready for action
second letter in 'explosive'
kisses
crossed swords
noughts & crosses
stop

A cross is a definite mark.
It can mean any of this list.
It is a symbol that has appeared
frequently in all of my work,
as a means of making a mark.
Am I signing my work in an
'I was here' kind of way or am
I endeavouring to maintain an
anonymity? Symbols appear in
all of our work, very often
without us recognizing them.
Only disinterested observers see
the truth. A friend once said to
me, 'Did you realize that all of
your work contains the colour
purple?' The X mark appears in
the same way.

RIGHT: This piece was created
using a thin wash of oil paint
on paper, creating layers of
colour and transparency.
Cross (Oil on paper, 1991)
76 x 38cm (30 x 15in)

APPENDIX

	Dip dye (hot-water acid dye)	Sublimation (transfer) dye	Heat tool	Soldering iron	Acrylic paint	Dye-based spritzes	Inkjet (dye) inks	Inkjet (pigment) ink	Printing aids (non acrylic)	Printing aids (acrylic)	Melting points	Composition	Construction
Lutradur 17, 30, 50, 70, 100, 130 and 230gsm	X	✓	✓	✓	✓	3	3	✓	✓	4	200ºC (392ºF)	5	8
Lutradur 300gsm	X	✓	✓	✓	✓	✓	X	X	✓	✓	200ºC (392ºF)	5	10
Crystal Spunbonded 17 and 70gsm	X	✓	✓	✓	✓	✓	3	3	✓	4	200ºC (392ºF)	5	8
Evolon 60, 80, 100, 130 and 170gsm	✓	✓	2	2	✓	3	3	✓	✓	4	230ºC (446ºF)	7	11
Heat-distressable Tissue 30gsm	X	✓	✓	✓	✓	3	3	✓	✓	2	200ºC (392ºF)	5	12
Nappy Liner 17, 30, 40, 50 and 100gsm	X	1	✓	✓	✓	3	3	✓	✓	4	70ºC (158ºF)	6	9
Tyvek Soft Structure (fabric) 43gsm	X	1	✓	✓	✓	3	3	✓	✓	4	200ºC (392ºF)	5	8
Tyvek Hard Structure Light (paper) 43 and 55gsm	X	1	✓	✓	✓	3	3	✓	✓	4	200ºC (392ºF)	5	8
Tyvek Hard Structure Medium (paper) 76gsm	X	1	✓	✓	✓	3	3	✓	✓	4	200ºC (392ºF)	5	8
Tyvek Hard Structure Heavy (paper) 105 and 110gsm	X	1	✓	✓	✓	3	3	✓	✓	4	200ºC (392ºF)	5	8
Kunin Felt 170gsm	X	X	✓	✓	✓	3	3	X	X	X	200ºC (392ºF)	5	10

1 These fabrics may shrink before sublimation process is complete – use with caution
2 Longer linger time required
3 Printing aid required for deeper colour
4 Will leave stiff residue
5 100% polyester

6 100% polypropylene
7 70% polyester 30% nylon
8 Thermal bonded
9 Point bonded
10 Needlefelted
11 Spunlace
12 Wet laid staple fibres

SUPPLIERS

Note: not all weights of fabrics are readily available.

RETAIL AND ONLINE OUTLETS

Gallery Textiles
4a Canalside
Metal & Ores Industrial Estate
Hanbury Road
Stoke Prior
Bromsgrove
B60 4JZ
Tel: 01527 882288
Website: www.gallerytextiles.co.uk
E-mail: sales@gallerytextiles.co.uk
(For spunbonded fabrics, Print.Ability, Colsperse Bondaweb, dye-based spritzes, craft soldering irons, 3D expanding medium, transfer dyes, transfer foils, mica powders)

Graphicus
Unit 5
Carrosserie House
Harmire Enterprise Park
Barnard Castle
Co Durham
DL12 8XT
Tel: 01833 695958
Website: www.graphicus.co.uk
(For rubber stamps, inkpads, Elusive Images CD-ROM and other crafting items)

Colourcraft (C&A) Ltd
Unit 5
555 Carlisle Street East
Sheffield
S4 8DT
Tel: 0114 242 143
Website: www.colourcraftltd.com
(For Aztec metallic paint, fabric paint, 3D expanding medium, dyes)

Spunart UK Ltd
1 Park Street
Allestree
Derby
DE22 2DR
Tel: 01332 554610
Website: www.spunart.co.uk
(Wholesale enquiries only, for Lutradur and Evolon)

WORKSHOPS

Wendy Cotterill at Gallery Textiles
For details of workshops for individuals or groups, e-mail wendy@gallerytextiles.co.uk or telephone 01527 882288. Current workshops are listed at gallery textiles.co.uk and are available as a PDF to download.

FURTHER READING

Blacklow, Laura, *New Dimensions in Photo Processes: A Step-by-Step Manual* (Focal Press, 1995)

Laury, Jean Ray, *Imagery on Fabric: A Complete Surface Design Handbook* (C&T Publishing, 1997)

Reed, Martin and Jones, Sarah, *Silver Gelatin: A Users Guide to Photographic Emulsions* (Argentum, 2001)

Webb, Randall and Reed, Martin, *Spirits of Salts: Working Guide to Old Photographic Processes* (Argentum, 1999)

Cloth Paper Scissors Magazine
www.clothpaperscissors.com

Craftsman Magazine: Craft & Design
Regular features include textiles and needlecraft directory, UK craft guide, craft courses and workshops, craft events, supplies and business information for practising artists. Published six times a year.

Selvedge Magazine
Magazine for designers and makers, published six times a year. See www.selvedge.org.

Stitch with the Embroiderers' Guild
Published six times a year. See www.embroiderersguild.com/stitch

WEBSITES

Lutradur.co.uk
Features information, experimental techniques projects, samples, and extra information on supplies as well as new developments in spunbonded fabrics and details of their availability.

For anyone interested in exploring the world of textiles and textile artists:

Workshop on the Web
www.workshopontheweb.com

Committed to Cloth
www.committedtocloth.com

Edge
www.edge-textileartists-scotland.com

Embroiderers' Guild
www.embroiderersguild.org.uk

HotHive Textiles
www.thetextiledirectory.com

South West Textiles
www.southwesttextilegroup.org.uk

Stitch Textile Artists
www.stitchtextileartists.co.uk

The Sixty Two Group of Textile Artists
www.62group.org.uk

Surface Design Association, USA
www.surfacedesign.org

Textile Study Group
www.textilestudygroup.co.uk

GALLERIES

All the galleries listed below regularly hold textile-related exhibitions as well as providing information and opportunities for practising artists.

New Brewery Arts
Brewery Court
Cirencester
GL7 1JH
Tel: 01285 657 181
Website: www.newbreweryarts.org.uk
Open seven days a week. Mon–Sat: 9am–5pm;
Sun: 10am–4pm
(Café, galleries, courses, information for makers, and shop.)

Ferrers Gallery
Staunton Harold
Ashby de la Zouch
Leicestershire
LE65 1RU
Tel: 01332 863337
Website: www.ferrersgallery.co.uk
Open Tues–Sun 10.30am–5pm
(Changing displays and exhibitions of British contemporary craft and applied arts, numerous craft workshops and tearoom.)

Farfield Mill
Garsdale Road
Sedbergh
Cumbria
LA10 5LW
Tel: 015396 21958
Website: www.farfieldmill.org
Open seven days a week, 10.30am–5.00pm
(Arts and heritage centre housed in a restored Victorian woollen mill. Heritage displays, working looms, regularly changing exhibitions, craft demonstrations, art and crafts for sale by resident and visiting artists, workshops, events and café.)

INDEX